WARWICKSHIRE

1 (overleaf) *Tredington spire in the Stour Valley*

VIVIAN BIRD

WARWICKSHIRE

B. T. Batsford Ltd
London

I dedicate this book to my grandson
Jason Langridge
in the hope that he will attain his
Golden Fleece without the perils
encountered by his classical namesake

First published 1973
© Vivian Bird 1973

Text printed in Great Britain by Northumberland Press
Ltd, Gateshead, Co. Durham. Plates printed and books
bound by Richard Clay (The Chaucer Press) Ltd, Bungay,
Suffolk for the publishers B. T. Batsford Ltd, 4 Fitz-
hardinge Street, London W1H 0AH

ISBN 0 7134 0076 5

CONTENTS

ACKNOWLEDGMENT

The Author and Publisher would like to thank the following for their kind permission to use photographs: Barnaby's Picture Library (15, 16, 20); J. Allan Cash (10, 21); Noel Habgood (frontispiece, 23); A. F. Kersting (8, 9, 12, 17, 19, 22, 24, 31); Popperfoto and G. F. Allen (14); Kenneth Scowen (2, 3, 7, 13, 28). 4, 5, 11, 18, 25-7, 29 and 30 are from the Publisher's collection. The map of Warwickshire is by permission of Patrick Leason.

LIST OF ILLUSTRATIONS

Introduction

Writing a book on Warwickshire while the proposals for local government reform were under consideration could have been a nerve-racking experience. Beset with change in so many things, in coinage, temperature, telephone numbers, postal district numbers, metrication—all changes for the worse—the topographical author, faced with radical changes in his chosen field, might well have sold his typewriter.

In general I deplore the changes in local government boundaries and nomenclature. In particular, where this book on Warwickshire is concerned, I welcome them and use them.

How much space should I devote to Birmingham and Coventry I asked the publishers when submitting a synopsis of chapters. As much or as little as you feel desirable was the reply.

My question arose from two considerations. I did not feel I could do justice to Birmingham and Coventry leaving sufficient room to do justice also to the remainder of Warwickshire; nor did I think that people buy a book on Warwickshire in order to read about two cities. There are books on Birmingham and books on Coventry. All my inclination was to leave them both out of this book.

Then the local government reformers, in their wisdom, excluded Birmingham and Coventry from Warwickshire, including them instead in a new West Midlands Metropolitan County. This was my cue to follow my inclination and exclude them from this book. But, just to emerge in my true colours, as a diehard traditionalist opponent of change, I have included Solihull—the 'Rus in Urbe' of the borough motto; the rural dormitory jam in the industrial sandwich between Birmingham and Coventry.

After all, if I must rationalize, whoever added 'Warwickshire' to any address in Birmingham or Coventry? Yet it has always been 'Solihull, Warwickshire'.

Introduction

At the time of writing another dormitory of Birmingham, the Royal Borough of Sutton Coldfield, is protesting feverishly at its possible merger with Birmingham, the main worry of loyal Sutton-ians being that Birmingham's deplorable mania for building wherever it can lay its rapacious hands on a green spot poses a terrible threat to the glorious expanse of Sutton Park. This magnificent, and still largely untamed breezy open space of 2,400 acres with its seven pools, its woodlands, and its heather—a constant heartbreak to the would-be builders in Birmingham—was given to Bishop Vesey by Henry VIII in 1528, and bequeathed by the bishop to the people of Sutton Coldfield.

To it in 1957 came 31,500 Scouts to celebrate the centenary of their founder, Lord Baden Powell, and many must feel nostalgic when —and if—in their 87 countries they ever smell the fragrance of hot sun on heather, gorse, and bracken, which is my abiding memory of Sutton Park.

John Vesey, born in Sutton in 1452, became Bishop of Exeter in 1519, accompanied Henry VIII to the Field of the Cloth of Gold, and was tutor to Mary Tudor. Retiring to Sutton in his seventies, in 1540 he founded Bishop Vesey's Grammar School—which takes pride in two V.Cs of the First World War—and, dying in his 103rd year, is buried in Sutton Coldfield Parish Church, where he lies mitred in effigy. Though he introduced kersey weaving to Sutton, built 51 houses for the weavers, paved the streets, and erected the Moot Hall, the bishop's great benefaction to his own and future generations was the grant of Sutton Park, and may any official of a future Birmingham Metropolitan District who vandalizes the park for housing be cursed by bell, book, and candle.

Along a pebbly ridge in Sutton Park runs a track: the Icknield Street practically as the Romans made it, a priceless possession to be guarded from the twentieth-century developers, of whose roads Warwickshire has enough and to spare. Recently a Birmingham newspaper described the city as 'the motorway hub of England', seemingly proud that it should be so. Warwickshire has suffered more than any other county that the boast may be made. Adequate roads have been 'improved' to the bewilderment and dismay of lovers of the county. Particular instances are the widening of the Alcester road with a consequent rape of thousands of trees and many acres of farmland, the threat of similar maltreatment alongside the A41 between Warwick and Banbury, and the substitution at several points of extensive and nerve-racking archipelagoes for straightforward islands or junctions.

Too much of the county that lives by the car from the factories of Coventry and Birmingham has already perished by the car, though there are still large unspoiled tracts with leafy lanes and charming villages comparable with any other county in Britain.

There is no better way of knowing a county than walking round its boundary. Some years ago I beat the bounds of Warwickshire to produce a series of articles in my newspaper. The perimeter of Warwickshire extends some 240 miles, and breaks up conveniently into six sections of common border with its neighbours—twelve days' walking at 20 miles a day. The features of the border prevail for some distance into the county—farming, potato growing, and sheep-rearing on the Leicester border, then a coalfield until one reaches the Northampton border which rises to uplands still grazed by sheep. Warwickshire marches with Oxfordshire on rust-coloured ironstone country much of which has been surface mined and returned to agriculture several feet below its original elevation. From the Cotswold outliers lapping over from Gloucestershire with their honey-coloured building stone, Warwickshire falls into the Avon valley where tidy regiments of orchard trees advance into Worcestershire. Only the Stafford border is built up, where the Black Country shoulders it with Birmingham, though the characteristics of these two individual areas, and of their people, are vastly different, and from Tamworth north-eastward our Stafford neighbour shares with us a more pastoral aspect.

Warwickshire is exceptionally rich in history, from its Roman roads to its having provided the First World War commander-in-chief, Haig, through residence, and, through the county regiment, Montgomery of Second World War fame. It has its own great battle in Edgehill, and across Warwickshire armies have marched in other wars to decisive battles just beyond its borders at Evesham in 1265 and Bosworth in 1485.

A topographical book inevitably relies for facts on the earlier works of others, and my acknowledgments go to previous writers on Warwickshire whom I have read over the years. I should, however, feel this book unjustified were I not able to introduce many new items on Warwickshire, sought out in my work as a journalist, and I thank the editor of the *Sunday Mercury* for permission to draw upon much that I learned while writing in his columns.

My thanks are again due to my friend, Norman Williams, for reading and correcting yet another book typescript for me—he has made his own mark on Warwickshire by shooting in the county pistol team.

CHAPTER ONE

The Stour Valley and Ilmington

Little Compton has two particular claims to distinction. It is the southernmost village in Warwickshire, which seems a fair reason for starting this book there, and it has a memorial window to the king who lost his head in a church dedicated to a saint who lost his head. Fourteen hundred years separated the executions of the two men, but they have come together in adjacent windows in this church, so close to the manor house that its saddleback tower merges with the secular gables and dormers in a symphony of stone, pale yellow in the sunlight, grey-brown in shadow.

St. Denis, patron saint of Paris, was beheaded on the hill since associated with anything but saintly behaviour—Montmartre. Legend relates that he picked up his head and carried it for burial at the site where the abbey of St. Denis has since risen. Churches usually depict him as a headless bishop carrying a mitred head. Somewhat inhibited, Little Compton portrays him wearing his head but holding a symbolic mitre. The dedication arises from an old association with Deerhurst Priory, near Tewkesbury, which was dependent on the Abbey of St. Denis at Paris—though Little Compton's spelling is St. Denys.

King Charles I was beheaded in Whitehall on 30 January 1649, and Little Compton Church illustrates three episodes from his last days; his farewell to his children, his walk in the snow, and his appearance on the scaffold, while a fourth subject shows his coffin carried into St. George's Chapel, Windsor. In each of these windows his friend and comforter appears—William Juxon, Bishop of London. After the execution Juxon retired to the manor house at Little Compton which he had inherited from Thomas Juxon, probably his brother.

So the martyr king was an appropriate subject, along with the martyr saint, for the windows given by Mrs. Gertrude Leverton Harris, who occupied Juxon's manor house from 1927 to 1938. A pity that this benefactress should have introduced a jarring note into this lovely place—the ugly oversized lettering by Eric Gill on her husband's tombstone.

Deprived of his see after the execution, Juxon devoted his time mainly to hunting with his own pack, said to exceed 'all other hounds in England for the pleasure and orderly hunting of them'. He used to walk to Chastleton, across the Oxford border, to divine service, and a proud possession of Chastleton House is the King's Bible from which Juxon read to Charles before his execution. Juxon kept deer at Little Compton Manor, and there is a small herd in the grounds today, the last direct descendant of the bishop's herd dying only recently.

With the leaves turning saffron and red there is no better introduction to Warwickshire than this charming manor house bathed in the mellow sun of a September afternoon, a house enshrining national and domestic history beneath those three frontal gables with their stone ball finials.

The road northward from Little Compton climbs on to Barton Hill, southernmost hill in Warwickshire, the Pisgah for the Promised Land ahead. On that hilltop, particularly when autumn puts a bloom on the hedgerow sloes, and spreads a quilt of golden grain, tawny stubble, and green pasture across the Stour Valley below, the Warwickshire man can feel proud of his county's beauty—a friendly rolling beauty. Down to the left of the dark mass of Wolford Wood stands the Four Shire Stone, now, with Worcestershire receded, the meeting place only of Gloucestershire, Oxfordshire, and Warwickshire.

Gloucestershire closes that view westward where the northern Cotswolds thrust one outlier into Warwickshire, the whaleback of Ilmington Downs where the county reaches its highest point of 854 feet. Against its bulk but closer to hand cluster the saddleback church tower and the yellow chimneys of the manor house at Barton-on-the-Heath. The spires of Great Wolford and Todenham, identical at this distance, alternately appear and are lost as shine or shade engulfs them. Eight miles away Tredington spire marks a church with evidence of doorways high above ground level, through which the

16

2 *Rainclouds over St. Swithin's Church, Lower Quinton*

3 *Half-timbering at Preston-on-Stour beside Alscot Park*

4 *Busts of six Roman emperors adorn the façade of seventeenth century Honington Hall*

5 *Honington's classical church*

Saxons took refuge from marauding Danes.

Past Tredington Church the River Stour flows northward to its confluence with the Avon near Stratford, and east of its valley Brailes Hill flaunts its tree-crest above Lower Brailes Church—the 'Cathedral of the Feldon'. The Feldon is that area of Warwickshire south of Stratford where large fields predominate, as against Arden, north of the Avon, famed for its woodlands.

Fold upon fold of wooded hills run down eastward of Barton Hill to the Oxford road before it ascends the ridge behind Long Compton to leave the county. On that ridge, flanked by conifer plantations, is the mysterious circle of the Rollright Stones known as the King's Men. They are in Oxfordshire, but across the road, the county boundary, their chief had stepped to the edge of the scarp to savour that exquisite panorama of south Warwickshire. There he stands to this day, the King Stone, petrified cobra-headed by a witch who, on that breezy height, offered him a kingdom.

> *If Long Compton thou canst see,*
> *King of England shalt thou be.*

Though he could see that wider view northward, the unfortunate chief was unsighted of Long Compton by the steepness of the scarp, and the other half of the witch's prophesy was fulfilled:

> *Rise up stick, stand still stone,*
> *For King of England thou shalt be none.*
> *Thou and thy men hoar stones shall be,*
> *And I myself an elder tree.*

So the chief, his 60 odd men, and a group of five 'Whispering Knights' face eternity on that ridge eastward of Barton Hill. The farmer on whose land the Rollright Stones stand told me he believed they were connected with the sacrifice of prisoners. A noted astronomer believes them to be calendrical. Having visited stone circles throughout the British Isles, he has observed that single stones outside them stand North 27 degrees East from the centre, and would, when the circles were established, point to the star Capella at dawn on the spring equinox, warning that it was time to sow crops.

At midnight on Hallowe'en the Rollright Stones are the resort of various wags, and the immediate countryside shrills with eldritch cackling as though witches are abroad. I know, because I have been there but I have an excuse, for my birthday is on Hallowe'en, which is said to give me an affinity with the witches.

Long Compton, across the fields east of Barton Hill, has a tradition of witchcraft, and once mustered 'enough witches to pull a cart up Long Compton Hill', though they would be choked by diesel fumes today from the busy main road between Stratford and the Oxford car industry. On 15 September 1875 a Long Compton farmhand, James Haywood, killed a 79-year-old woman, Ann Tennent, with a pitchfork, because he thought she was a witch along with 15 other Long Compton women. The village has always been a place of tall stories, one of the earliest concerning St. Augustine. Preaching at the church, Augustine was told that the lord of the manor refused to pay his tithes, so the saint excommunicated him. He declared that no excommunicated person should be present at Mass, whereupon a dead man, buried just inside the church, rose from his grave and walked into the churchyard. Questioning the 'dead man' afterwards, Augustine learned that he, too, had been excommunicated for non-payment of tithes, 150 years earlier.

There is reference to 'Man Friday' in Long Compton Church, the Sheldon's 'Man Friday'. The Sheldons were a great family from Weston Park nearby, once the richest commoners in England. In the porch is preserved a broken headstone with the inscription: 'In memory of Joseph Friday, who after having served the late Edward Sheldon Esq. and his family above 40 years died 5 October 1746, aged 55.' The lych-gate at Long Compton Church has a thatched upper room, bought and restored from its previously neglected state by George Kinsey Latham. On his death in 1964 the room was given by Mrs. Marion Latham as a memorial to her husband. From a studio at Long Compton Donald Brooke, an artist in stained glass, sends out his work far and wide. An earlier example of village craftsmanship was the King's Stone Printing Press, set up in 1922 by the Rev. William Manton, which, during the General Strike in 1926, published the *Long Compton Wireless News*, distributed throughout England by drivers passing through the village. Long Compton had its Victorian venture in social security. The Long

6   *Gerard Johnston's half-length figure of Shakespeare above the spot where the poet is buried in Holy Trinity chancel at Stratford-upon-Avon*

7 *The Wilmcote home of Shakespeare's mother, Mary Arden's House,
is an interesting folk museum*

Compton Assurance Society, founded in 1869, with 34 members, rose to 138 by 1900, and when its banner was displayed at a village exhibition in its centenary year it still claimed 38 adherents.

To the east of Long Compton rises Whichford Wood where, searching as though for a needle in a haystack, the diligent hunter can find the most remote memorial in Warwickshire. In June 1916 a Corporal Ivens, home on leave, had gone with some woodmen friends who were working in the wood. There, learning of the loss of Earl Kitchener of Khartoum in H.M.S. *Hampshire*, he carved on a beech trunk 'K. of K., Drowned 6-6-16, R.I.P.' With the years the incisions have spread so that now they are of considerable size— though the date should have been 5 June 1916. To reach the tree I took the Hook Norton road from Whichford with the wood a mere bristle to westward. After half a mile I turned right at a track sign-posted 'Doctor's Barn', some farm buildings named after a Dr. Yeomans, Rector of Whichford, who got a generous slice of land through the Enclosure Act about 1806. The track led to a path just inside the southern fringe of the wood, and along it, among other trees, an occasional beech spread its branches towards the open field. The fifth or sixth bore the inscription, hidden from the path.

The road down Barton Hill enters Barton-on-the-Heath near the steps into the churchyard. The first headstone on the right of the path commemorates a deputy lieutenant of Warwickshire, Cecil Henry Howkins, who died on Hallowe'en, 1947, and 'whose ashes are scattered on Barton Hill'. He obviously loved that spacious view and has involved himself with it. Can man come closer to immortality?

A quaint pig has trodden a lonely road in effigy across the chancel arch at Barton since Norman times, and early this century a memorial tablet was dedicated to Lance Corporal Gerard Nettleship, killed on 6 January 1900 in Ladysmith during the siege. Across the north wall of the churchyard is Barton House, a beautiful early seventeenth-century building. Captain Robert Dover (1575-1641), who pioneered the Cotswold Games on Dover's Hill on the Cotswold Edge, was an attorney at Barton, and the village is mentioned in *The Taming of the Shrew*: 'Am I not Christopher Sly, old Sly's son of Bartonheath ... by present profession a tinker?' Shakespeare should have known Barton well for it was the home of his cousins, the Lamberts.

North of Barton and of Great and Little Wolford a salient of Gloucestershire reaches eastward to Mitford Bridge on the A34, where the River Stour changes its early westerly course and begins its northerly meanderings to the Avon. It has entered Warwickshire at Traitors Ford Lane, a prehistoric green road running from Edgehill to the Rollright Stones which does not live up to its exciting name, though Gallows Hill Farm beside it recalls that cattle thieves were once hanged there. Three miles downstream the Mill House at Stourton is admired by many with its wrought-iron peacock gates and the millrace cascading into the front garden to flow to Cherington where another mill ground corn for cattle fodder until 1948. North of the river are the Brailes villages, and to southward Weston Park, owned in the mid-sixteenth century by William Sheldon, a sheep dealer and wool stapler who had another estate at Beoley in Worcestershire, and, through his wife, Mary Willington, a third at Barcheston down the Stour. About 1554 he sent his elder son, Ralph, with Richard Hyckes of Barcheston, to the Continent. In Flanders they learned tapestry weaving, with the result that in 1561, having imported some Flemish weavers, William Sheldon set up looms at Barcheston and founded the industry associated with his name.

The venture prospered until the growing popularity of paper hangings killed it, but not before it had left a priceless legacy of craftsmanship. One woven series of county maps anticipated the Ordnance Survey in its symbols for churches. Birmingham University inherited some Barcheston tapestries from Lady Barber, and in 1919 eight pieces were found in the butler's room at Chastleton House, some of which are in the Victoria and Albert Museum. Both William Sheldon and Ralph died at Skilts, near Beoley, in 1570 and 1613 respectively. Later Sheldons, including William's great-great-grandson Ralph, 'The Great Sheldon' (1623-1684), died at Weston, but all were buried at Beoley.

Manor House Farm, Barcheston, where the tapestry industry was first established, still stands. It is thought that the looms were accommodated in a room running the length of the attic, used lately as a cheese room. One of the fields is called Town Ground, being the site of the old dwellings at Barcheston before the Flemish weavers moved to a rival tapestry industry at Mortlake, and the village was ultimately depopulated, probably by cholera. The newer centre of population is Willington, a mile away, where the older folk still talk of the Willington Wake and how 'Fiddler' Stirch played for the dancing. Barcheston has only the farm, the old rectory, and a couple of cottages—no inn, post office, shop, nor school. But its church still survives, consecrated on St. Martin's Day, 11 November, 1291, and it acknowledges its dedication to that saint with a west window telling the story of his life, and with a copy of Vandyke's famous picture of St. Martin. Outside is a stone to Richard Hyckes, the original weaver, who died in 1621, aged 97. Inside, in the south transept, is a fine alabaster memorial to William Willington, who helped the cholera depopulate the neighbourhood by turning out his tenants from their farms that sheep might flourish instead. He died in 1554, and lies piously in effigy with his wife Anne, who was previously married to Thomas Middlemore of Edgbaston, Birmingham.

Around the tomb are ranged their seven remarkable daughters, all of whom married well. Margery's first husband was a Thomas Holt of Aston; Anne married Francis Mountford of Kingshurst, Castle Bromwich, and two of Katherine's three husbands were from important Catholic families associated with the Gunpowder Plot—William Catesby of Lapworth and Anthony Throckmorton. But it was Mary, who by marrying William Sheldon, brought tapestry and fame to Barcheston. On the roads just south of Barcheston, one sees occasionally at junctions the old gatehouses of Weston Manor. They are now cottage dwellings, the drives are roads, and the great house of the Sheldons, after a rebuilding in 1832 by a George Phillips, was finally demolished in 1934.

For the end of the Sheldon story we seek a sepulchre in the churchyard of St. George's, Lower Brailes, the 'Cathedral of the Feldon'. In the south of the burial ground is the tomb of Edward Ralph Charles Sheldon (1782-1836) and his Irish wife Marcella. Three of their children who died in infancy are buried with them. Another son who survived them lies in the north-east of the churchyard beneath a stone surmounted spectacularly by six pillars supporting a canopy crowned by two winged sphinxes. The inscription rings down the curtain on the Sheldon family—'In loving memory of Henry James Sheldon of Brailes House, who died 24 December 1901, aged

78. This monument was erected by his only sister Isabel Calmady, the last of the Sheldons.'

Brailes Church shows evidence of religious toleration in an exterior inscription beneath the east window: 'Pray for the soul of the Rev. John Austin, for many years pastor to the Catholics of Brailes and neighbourhood. He died 27 August 1809, aged 68, R.I.P.' Today the Roman Catholic church of St. Peter and St. Paul must be sought in the manor house, built in 1726.

Tragedy came to Lower Brailes in 1876-7 when 37 children of the parish died of diphtheria. Their memorial is a window in the south aisle, and near it is a verse to Richard Davies, Gentleman, who died 19 January 1639, aged 36.

> *Though dead hee bee yet lives his fame,*
> *Like rose in June so smells his name.*
> *Rejoice we at his change, not faint,*
> *Death kild a man, but made a saint.*

During the past three years this area of south Warwickshire has produced its own writer in the remarkable person of Aubrey Seymour, who published his first book, *The Land Where I Belong* in 1969 at the age of 82, following it in 1970 with *Fragrant the Fertile Earth*. Mr. Seymour, whose home is now at Weston Mill on the Stour, has lived and farmed all his life hereabouts. I met him one January morning in 1969, a morning which was dead when I left my Birmingham home yet, by the time I turned off the Oxford road at a lodge of Weston Park, some glorious alchemy had wrought a transformation. Gone was the deadly grip of frost and fog. The day had been brought to life, the dead hand of winter lifted, and the voice of the west wind was loud in the land. I paused to take it all in, for it seemed the right atmosphere in which to approach Aubrey Seymour. Through windows in the purple-bellied clouds sunshafts lit up distant fields with that clean-bleached look of the early year. Trees stood out miles away on distant horizons, their tracery seen with remarkable clarity. It is surely one of winter's great compensations that trees take on personality when bare of the leaves which cloak them in summer anonymity. Mr. Seymour came to meet me across his lawn which was suffering an invasion by moles—'Mouldewarps or oonts we country-folk call them', he said—tall, bulky, up-right, deerstalker on head, and limping slightly from a riding mishap 50 years earlier.

The Knee Brook flows through many of Aubrey Seymour's pages, a tributary entering the Stour just north of Mitford Bridge. It forms the boundary between Warwickshire and Gloucestershire for two miles, during which it is crossed, near Todenham, by a stout concrete bridge inscribed 'To Beryl "Buck" from the War-wickshire Hunt, 1959'. Beryl Buckmaster was Master of the Hunt for nine years until 1958 when she chose the bridge as a retirement present.

North-eastward of Shipston-on-Stour the river flows through Fell Mill Farm where a fossilized ichthyosaurus has been unearthed of recent years, and where they still have a railed cockpit in the farm-house. Honington, downstream, has been placed high in competitions for Warwickshire's most beautiful village, though it has the less enviable distinction, on a memorial to Joseph Townsend in its church, of the ugliest cherub ever perpetrated by a monumental mason. On a splendid marble monument Sir Henry Parker and his son Hugh are said by Pevsner to be 'elegantly gesticulating'—each is lifting his skirts to show a saucy knee.

Tredington has two converted mills, vines from which wine has been made, and a church dedicated to St. Gregory with some Saxon work, and a spire which dominates the landscape. A consciously charming village, Tredington is a mellow place to wander on a sunny day. The Stour there is probably the first water seen by one who was to become famous as Admiral Sir Hyde Parker, commander of the British fleet in the Battle of Copenhagen, where he issued the signal to which Nelson turned his blind eye. Hyde Parker was born at Tredington, where his father was rector. Most of all, Tredington is famous for the antique shops, of which it has several.

The Stour flows from east to west of the A34 at the entrance to Ettington Park Hotel, one of the spots memorable to me for the sight of kingfishers. Stately cedars and wellingtonias rise from smooth lawns above the drive leading to the hotel's assembly of Victorian Gothic turrets completed in 1862. This exciting building, the colour of old mustard, and assuming an eerie quality as dusk embraces it, celebrated its centenary by providing an autumn setting

27

in 1962 for the film, *The Haunting*, starring Claire Bloom and Richard Johnson.

When Domesday Book was completed the lords of the manor of Ettington were the Shirleys who trace their lineage direct from Saxon times, the oldest family in England. Their present seat is in Ireland, but they are still 'overlords' of Ettington, which is adorned liberally with their saracen's head crest in memory of Sir Thomas Shirley's participation in the Crusades, and the horseshoes of the Ferrers of Staunton Harold, Leicestershire, whose heiress, a Shirley, married in the fifteenth century. A frieze of 14 panels around the exterior of Ettington Hall summarizes the Shirley saga which began when Henry Sewallis, who died about 1129, took the name of Shirley from a Derbyshire village near Ashbourne where he married a local lady. A Sir Ralph, who died in 1327, and lies in effigy with his wife Margaret at Ettington, was M.P. for Warwick, as was his son, Thomas, who fought in the French Wars of Edward III. Sir Hugh, falconer to Henry IV, was killed at the Battle of Shrewsbury in 1403, one of four knights wearing similar armour to the king for his greater protection. Hugh's son, Ralph, fought valiantly for Henry V, but missed Agincourt through illness, though his eight esquires and 18 archers were there. It was Ralph's son, another Ralph, who married as the first of his three wives the heiress of Staunton Harold Hall, which became the Shirleys' principal estate. His grandson, yet another Ralph, married four times.

George Shirley was created a baronet in 1611, the year when James I established the order, and his son, Sir Henry, married a daughter of Queen Elizabeth's favourite, the Earl of Essex. This gave subsequent Shirleys the right to quarter the Royal Arms, as the Essex family was descended from Richard Plantagenet, grandson of Edward III. Their son, Sir Robert, was committed to the Tower by Cromwell in 1656 after he had built the church at Staunton Harold, the only one to be built during the Commonwealth.

'If he can afford to build a church he can afford to supply a ship', said the Cromwellians, but, a faithful Royalist, Robert went instead to the Tower, to die 'not without suspicion of poison'.

The father-figure of this fascinating family is undoubtedly his son, Robert Shirley, created Earl Ferrers by Queen Anne in 1711. He married twice, first Elizabeth Washington of Wiltshire by whom he had 17 children, and second Selina Finch of London who bore him 10 more—a grand total of 27, to which must be added at least 30 illegitimate. After these astonishing feats of fecundity he died in 1717. His titles went to his eldest surviving son by his first wife, together with his Staunton Harold estate. Ettington went to a son by his second marriage, George, an outsize egotist who had an enormous monument constructed to his parents, with them standing modestly on either side while he sprawls across the top—the showpiece of the ruined church at Ettington, the second Earl Ferrers having refused it a place at Staunton Harold, where he had installed a more seemly memorial to his father who is buried there. The egregious George is interred at Ettington along with his son George, who emulated his grandfather by marrying twice, but had no issue by either wife.

While the Ettington Shirleys were quietening down the senior line at Staunton Harold was producing a colourful 4th Earl Ferrers. Divorced for cruelty, he shot dead the steward sent to collect rents settled on his wife. Arrested, tried, and sentenced to death, Ferrers set out on his last journey from the Tower to Tyburn on 5 May 1760, travelling in his own landau drawn by six horses, and wearing his wedding suit of white silk. It was an impressive prelude to a new method of hanging, for there was no undignified push off a cart for the earl. For him it was the trapdoor and the drop—his lordship was the pioneer of death from the modern scaffold.

Below the church tower at Ettington there is a long archaic rhyming epitaph giving 'a true report upon the death of Anthony Underhill, who died 16 July 1587.' Seemingly he had a vision at the moment of death, with spectators vouching for his ecstary.

Whose glorious death, and happy end was such
Which twentie sawe, that did rejoice them much.
For when the tyme of's fatall houre drew neare
Rose up with joye, a vision he espies,
Behold, quoth he, for yonder doth appeare
My Saviour Christ, I see him with myne eyes.

There is much more, but in a dog's graveyard at Ettington a humble stone provides an outstanding epitaph. It stretches across two small mounds:

29

Here Nelson lies by Tory's grave,
Both dogs of high degree:
True to their name, both faithful, brave,
Tories are wont to be.

The road from Tredington to Ettington by-passes Halford just to the east, its church having a Norman doorway where a quaint face, upside down, looks from one capital at a man grasping a beast by its open jaws on another, while in the tympanum above an angel has its arms outstretched seemingly in the homely act of holding out a skein of wool. The interior incorporates a Norman chancel arch, eight capitals carved with different leaves, two fire hooks for tearing down burning thatch, and a fourteenth-century treble bell, probably the oldest inscribed bell in Warwickshire.

A fourteenth-century toll house remained at Halford until about 1870 when it was removed stone by stone and re-erected at Shottery. At the junction of the Fosse Way and the Idlicote road in Halford it was as lucrative a toll as any in the county, commanding the busy traffic between Leamington and Bath when it was fashionable to 'take the waters'. A land surveyor, Thomas Webb, employed around Halford on the field enclosures in 1774-5 spent all the profit from his appointment in building a house resembling 'the upright knife-box of the period'. It has two octagonal towers side by side, with a winding stair in the angle between them at the back, and is called The Folly.

Opposite Ettington Park stands a pillar with a rhyme:

Six miles to Shakespeare's town whose fame
Is known o'er all the earth,
To Shipston four, whose lesser fame
Boasts no such poet's birth.

This elaborate milestone stands where a byway leaves the A34, a pleasant route west of the Stour to Preston, much of it unfenced. At one point a footpath strikes off to the church at Whitchurch which rears its tower from the fields, a twin to Alderminster tower across the river. Ursula Bloom, the novelist, has written about Whitchurch, where her father was rector.

Insignificant though it is, the Stour provides so formidable a barrier that St. Mary's, Whitchurch, stands barely 400 yards from Alderminster Church, the two serving communities divided by the river. Alderminster has had a church since the fifth century when the settlement, then called Aeldrehame, was a mile northward up the Stratford road from the site of the present church, where in those days stood a village known after the river as Sture. By 549 this southern settlement had a convent, or minster, and in 843 the growth of population merited the promotion of the convent chapel to the status of parish church of Aeldredstureminster. This church was demolished by the Normans, who raised in its place a building they deemed more worthy, and the present nave is part of that Norman church. In 1193 the minster became a priory of Pershore Abbey and the Norman chancel was in turn fetched down to make way for the tower, transepts and new chancel at a time when the rounded Norman was turning to the pointed arch of Early English architecture.

Alderminster's development has not all been peaceful. The Danes came along one day and killed the priest, and in 1349 stark tragedy struck with the Black Death, when every inhabitant of the northern settlement of Aeldrehame died of plague or hunger.

Around Alderminster, beside the A34, the perceptive traveller sees much evidence of the horse tramway from Stratford to Moreton-in-Marsh, Gloucestershire, which opened on 5 September 1826. The line was the dream of engineer William James of Henley-in-Arden, the first 16 miles of a Central Junction Railway which he proposed continuing to London via Oxford, thus linking a busy inland canal and river dock at Stratford with the capital. Its route follows the main road to Newbold, where it struck west across country almost to Ilmington, turning south towards Darlingscott, and passing the Old Wharf and Junction House, still identifiable east and south-east of Ilmington. The tramway company ceased its separate existence in 1869 and later the Great Western Railway used 8½ miles of the old track for its new line from Moreton to Shipston. Demolition of this line began in 1961, but its route can still be traced, marked by houses with neat porches at the level crossings—one, in particular, at Darlingscott.

Preston-on-Stour, a pretty village, is an obvious appendage to the 'big house' in Alscot Park, home of the West family, which has a large herd of deer. For some years a late January walk, beginning and ending at Stratford, with a lunch stop at the 'Fox', Loxley, and a search for aconites in a wood at Ettington, took in Preston Church, where we never failed to wonder at the well-displayed charms of several ladies in the Dutch glass of the east window, which must often have turned the celebrant's mind to more worldly things than Holy Communion. That walk, always well patronized, continued back to Stratford by a fine field path from Atherstone-on-Stour to Clifford Chambers, a path I never tread without seeing George Welch, who always led that ramble, and Alderman Jack Wood, a fine writer on walking, both around six feet four inches, striding ahead as I hope they still step out together in the Elysian Fields.

That January walk usually took us through Clifford Chambers in a frosty dusk. August and September are the months to see the village in the opulence of its colourful gardens—a backwater blessed by the fact that its long wide street is a cul-de-sac, closed to traffic at the end by the Manor House, described by Michael Drayton as 'the muse's quiet port', with the exquisite timber-framed rectory nearby.

Shortly after the Second World War a Hungarian named Tibor Reich settled in Clifford Chambers Mill to experiment in producing deep-texture furnishing fabric. The venture prospered; Tibor fabric goes all over the world and has been used in Coventry Cathedral and aboard the *Queen Elizabeth II* along with other great liners, and is always on display in an exhibition room in Ely Street, Stratford.

A mile beyond Clifford Chambers the Stour comes to its confluence with the Avon, but from the village we will turn south down the A48 to take in the Ilmington area, beginning at Lower Quinton, where St. Swithun's Church always draws me like a magnet to the pageant of local history glowing from the heraldic glass in its modern windows. While savouring the thatched-cottage charm of the village the visitor becomes aware of heraldry in the sign of the College Arms, blazoning the lilies and ermine lozenges of Magdalen College, Oxford, large landowners in the vicinity.

Lower Quinton Church owes its origin to the nuns of Polesworth, far away across Warwickshire, where St. Edith was the abbess— 'quean' from which Quinton derives, was Saxon for 'woman'. Edith's brother, King Ethelwulf, was a pupil of Swithun, hence the dedication. The Rev. Gordon H. Poole, vicar from 1911 to 1932, who beautified the church with the windows, and Geoffrey Webb, the stained-glass artist, asked the village schoolchildren if there was anything they would like included, and, as a result, a close scrutiny reveals butterflies, insects, elves in snail shells, an owl, a wren, a swallow, and other birds. The arms include those of the Marmions —a Polesworth association; the Loggins of Wincote, a house north of Quinton where it is thought *The Taming of the Shrew* was first played; the wyvern of the Brents of Lark Stoke; and the garbs and scallop shells of the Edens, which still appear in the arms of Lord Avon, who, as Sir Anthony Eden, was M.P. for Warwick and Leamington.

The three stars argent on a field sable of the Overburys takes my mind to the manor house of Admington, two miles away, where once they lived, and on beyond Ilmington Downs to drop eventually to Compton Scorpion Manor, once the home of Sir Thomas Overbury, uncle of another Thomas Overbury who lies in Quinton Church. A courtier and a minor poet, the uncle was the victim 350 years ago of the blackest crime in the history of Warwickshire, though it was played out in the Tower of London.

James I, notorious for his handsome male favourites, looked with pleasure on a certain unworthy Robert Carr, who had all the graces except brains. For these he relied on his friend Overbury, so successfully that he became Viscount Rochester. Frances Howard, wife of the Earl of Essex, fell in love with Rochester, and not content with using love potions and witchcraft to gain his affection, she wanted to divorce Essex and marry Rochester. Overbury was perfectly content to condone Rochester's affair with Frances, and even wrote Rochester's love-letters to her. But at their marrying he drew the line, sensing that it would oust him from Rochester's favour. Frances was enraged at this opposition, and offered a friend £1,000 to pick a fight with Overbury and kill him, but the friend declined. Rochester himself then plotted some villainy. Knowing the king to be jealous of Overbury for his place in Rochester's affections, Rochester persuaded James to offer Overbury a position abroad, advised Overbury to refuse it, then suggested to the king that the refusal constituted treason.

So James sent Overbury to the Tower, where the lieutenant was a friend of Frances. Through him she sent Overbury to a lingering death by a variety of poisons, so that he died on 14 September 1613. Meanwhile she was suing for divorce, and Essex was only too glad to be rid of such a hell-cat. She said that their marriage had not been consummated and, when the court asked her to be examined, the king himself, urged on by £25,000 from Rochester, substituted a woman he knew to be a virgin. The divorce was granted. Frances, still only 20, and Rochester were married and became Earl and Countess of Somerset. But with Buckingham's growing power they were deposed from James I's favour and tried for Overbury's murder. Found guilty, they were placed in perpetual imprisonment and grew to hate each other.

Upper Quinton, with a picturesque timbered manor house, is on the route to Meon Hill, a magnificent viewpoint across the Vale of Evesham, which invests the Quinton villages with an unsolved mystery which still causes eyes to be averted and lips closed to the inquisitive. On St. Valentine's Day, 1945, a farm labourer was found dead on Meon Hill pinned to the ground with his own pitch-fork through his throat, a so-called 'witchcraft murder' which has baffled all attempts to solve it.

The land falls from Meon Hill to the Mickleton-Ilmington road, to rise again to Ilmington Downs and a hoary old signpost at War-wickshire's highest point. Standing on a shelf in a combe on the downs is Lark Stoke's stone-built and mullioned manor house, dating from around 1600. It was a Richard Brent who erected the present house and who became Sheriff of Gloucestershire in 1614. The last Brents at Lark Stoke were three spinsters and their widowed sister, Dame Elizabeth Lytcott, who let out small holdings recalled long afterwards in field names, Newman's Close, Tilson's Close, Thompson's Close, and Underhill's Grounds. Dame Elizabeth sur-vived at Lark Stoke until 1768, and is remembered today by Madam's Pear Tree, with small strange-tasting fruit.

John Hart, who succeeded the Brents in the manor house, was a weaver of shag—a kind of plush—which brought temporary pros-perity to Shipston-on-Stour, where his bust is in the church. In 1875 one John Edwin Wilson took over the Lark Stoke estate, and it has now descended to his grandson George Wilson.

'My grandfather was the last shin-kicking champion at the Dovers Hill Games', George Wilson told me in December 1970. 'I was born here in the manor house 57 years ago, and took over 17 years back.'

Today Lark Stoke Farm spreads over 560 acres. One of Mr. Wilson's sons is responsible for all the arable; the other for the cattle.

'I'm pigs', said George. 'We always have at least 400 here. The only other employee is a part-time pensioner. Different from the days when we employed nine on 275 acres. The old threshing machine took nine men. Today two of us do the job. Years ago farming was a way of life, now it's a money-making business costed to decimal points of a penny. For each worker you pay £5 before you begin paying him. Daft, isn't it? We sow grain and spray our crops by air, and with our own airstrip on the downs it costs less because the pilot doesn't have to charge for a long run-in. My son, John, pilots his own aircraft, though not for agricultural purposes.'

'The time is coming', George concluded, 'when the farmer will merely supply the land and keep an eye on the livestock. Everything else will be done by contract firms. We are excavating an old mill pond below the house. Stocked with trout, and the fishing let at present prices, a four-acre pool will make double the profit of four acres of corn.'

Mr. Wilson also lets his fields on the slopes of the downs for twice-yearly motor cycle scrambles. On the way up the track through those fields to the breezy summit of Warwickshire we pass the remains of a barn where a farmer, John Southam, once tried to hang himself. His labourer found him and cut him down in time to save his life—only to find his next wages reduced by the cost of the rope.

CHAPTER TWO

Stratford-upon-Avon

Entering Stratford-upon-Avon the Shipston road crosses a railway with a separate footbridge to the left, leading to a footpath raised among the trees. This was the track of the Stratford-Moreton Tramway, and it makes a pleasant walk into the town skirting the cricket ground, with views beyond the riverside recreation ground of Holy Trinity Church and the Royal Shakespeare Theatre across the rippled stream of Avon. Immediately before the old tramway bridge crosses the river into Bancroft Gardens one of the trucks is preserved on a length of the metals. On the Shipston road is the Old Tramway Inn, its sign depicting the departure from Stratford of the horse tram. The horses were stabled at the inn.

At the southern end of Clopton Bridge with its 14 arches stands Alveston Manor Hotel. History proliferates at river crossings, and a Saxon community flourished on this southern bank of the Avon 500 years before Sir Hugh Clopton spanned the river with his bridge. In 1934 a pagan Saxon cemetery with 53 burials was excavated in a gravel pit adjacent to the manor grounds, and a new dig in 1970 revealed more skeletons. I was present as a young woman archaeologist scraped with her trowel around the pelvic region of a Saxon lady at a metal object which we thought might have been a chastity belt. It reminded me that beneath the magnificent cedar on the hotel lawn across the path several Titanias have lisped the lines, in open-air performances of *A Midsummer Night's Dream*:

> *The moon methinks looks with a watery eye;*
> *Lamenting some enforced chastity.*

Monks from Worcester built on the site of the present manor house, constructing also a first wooden bridge across the Avon, and a fishpond near the present Tiddington road connected with the river. The history of their house until the Dissolution around 1538 is recorded in the hotel's Cedar Room in stained glass fashioned by Donald Brooke. Concluding the manor's story a glass picture is captioned 'The Restoration of Alveston Manor by William Thomas Bird'. Mr. Bird has made a considerable impact on Stratford in his colourful rise from a Birmingham barrow boy to a wealthy and influential industrialist with worldwide connections. Here is his greatest monument for, in the Alveston glass, he is featured not only alongside SS. Oswald and Wulstan, both bishops of Worcester, but Queen Matilda and King Henry III.

Though the resident religious community was proscribed at the Dissolution, the Chapter of Worcester Cathedral was allowed to keep Alveston Manor at the cost of maintaining 12 divinity students, each of whom had to be allowed £6 7s. 6d. a year. To obtain release from this the Chapter gave the manor back to the Crown. Thus it began its secular life, among the various occupants being Ludovic Greville of the Earl of Warwick's family, and Sir Ambrose Cave, Chancellor of the Duchy of Lancaster to Elizabeth I.

It was after the Second World War that Mr. Bird moved in and refashioned the façade, using wood from scrapped Birmingham trams as window frames and timber from tank transporters as exterior beams. Eventually the manor was sold to Sir Charles Forte, and in his hotel today accommodation ranges from delightfully quaint raftered rooms to exquisite suites in the Queen Anne stables. The visitor is left in no doubt that he is in Shakespeare country. Among reminders of the Bard are two pictures in glass, one of Romeo climbing on to Juliet's balcony, the other Petruchio invested with a new hat for his wedding in *The Taming of the Shrew*. The Delft tiles of the lounge fireplace depict scenes such as Ariel 'on the bat's back I do fly'; Malvolio all cross-gartered in *Twelfth Night*; Titania making love to Bottom in his ass's head; Hermione's statue come to life in *The Winter's Tale*, Othello telling the tale to Brabantio and Desdemona, with other scenes from *King Lear*, *Macbeth*, and *Hamlet*.

Presiding on the front lawn is a statue of Shakespeare found in the back garden of a house in Kenilworth Road, Leamington Spa. Beside the lawn the Nut Walk can still be trodden, and the Monks'

Wall can be identified. At various times these were used as bowling alleys. In all, Alveston Manor is cradled in history, with Shakespearean memories crowding in as thick as the ghosts crowded in on Richard III in his tent before Bosworth Field.

Once in the manor grounds, but now on a traffic island, a charming Tudor gazebo faces along Clopton Bridge, a reminder of another Stratford gazebo in the grounds of Mason Croft, now the Shakespeare Institute, where Marie Corelli, the novelist who from 1899 to 1924 brought a purple patch to Stratford's scene, did her writing. Among her fancies were the Shetland ponies, Puck and Ariel, which pulled her chaise, and the gondola in which she was poled about the Avon by an imported gondolier, Giovanni—a memory I offer to future guests at the new Hilton Hotel on the riverside upstream of Clopton Bridge, as they are taken by boat to the Royal Shakespeare Theatre, which raises its own bulk beyond the Bancroft Gardens on the opposite side of the bridge. Familiarity is making the 'new' theatre acceptable to many who disliked Miss Elizabeth Scott's design when it was opened in 1932. Unsworth's original Memorial Theatre was burned down in 1926, though some of its Gothic flamboyance can still be seen in Waterside.

Bancroft Gardens is a pleasant place to wander before a theatre performance on a warm summer's evening. They gain character from the canal which looks down through them to the Avon, and on the Shakespeare Monument by Lord Ronald Gower the figures of Hamlet, Prince Hal, Falstaff, and Lady Macbeth are a reminder that Stratford's most famous son was, in his plays, a master of philosophy, history, comedy, and tragedy.

The visitor who would know something of Stratford's past can do worse than start at the Guild Chapel. Some atavistic streak often sends me back to my unlettered ancestors for whom pictorial church glass served as books, and here the east window, with its many legends, relates the ancient history of Stratford. This came home to me most vividly on a recent visit to the chapel when, with the representation in a window of John de Coutances, Bishop of Worcester, 1195-98, I read 'The weekly market secured by the Bishop in 1196 is still here. In 1818 it was altered from Thursday to Friday.' I then strolled up Scholars Lane and Rother Street and, it happening to be Friday, there, bridging 776 years in a three-

8 *Shakespeare's birthplace, Stratford-upon-Avon*

9 *Ann Hathaway's Cottage, Shottery*

minute walk, were the market stalls doing good business.

Driving often through Stratford I am always conscious of a degree of privilege when I reflect that all over the world, but particularly in the U.S.A., countless thousands are saving and scheming to be where the accident of birth and residence directs me so frequently. How these prospective pilgrims must envy some Stratfordians who look out daily from their shop doors, and better from their bedroom windows every morning on the half-timbered birthplace in Henley Street with its gables and latticed windows, its neat porch above the so oft trodden entrance, and the flag with Shakespeare's heraldic spear in a bend dexter sable.

In the book-lined graciousness of what has been described, as 'one of the most beautiful offices in the world' Dr. Levi Fox, O.B.E., contrives to function successfully as Director of the Shakespeare Birthplace Trust despite the international cavalcade constantly passing through the birthplace garden beneath his window in the Shakespeare Centre. Though the Trust and the Royal Shakespeare Theatre are both concerned to do honour to Shakespeare they are separate entities, the Trust by far the older. Pilgrims were visiting Stratford in the seventeenth century shortly after the poet's death, and by the mid-eighteenth century national appreciation had assumed such proportions that in 1756 the Rev. Francis Gastrell, owner of New Place, where Shakespeare died, first cut down the famous mulberry tree beneath which the poet sat in his later years, and three years later destroyed the house itself because of the inroads of visitors on his privacy.

Stratford was ultimately established as a shrine in 1769 when David Garrick organized the first major festival in Shakespeare's honour, a week of rejoicing, acting, and fireworks. The birthplace, then in private hands, was shamelessly exploited, but in 1847 it was offered for public auction and acquired as a national shrine. This was the beginning of the Trust, which has since acquired New Place gardens (1862), Anne Hathaway's Cottage at Shottery (1892), Mary Arden's House, Wilmcote (1930) and Hall's Croft, the Tudor home of Dr. John Hall, Shakespeare's son-in-law, and his daughter Susanna, in 1949. In 1964, the poet's quatercentenary was celebrated by the opening of the Shakespeare Centre adjoining the birthplace garden.

10   Cottages at Shottery: Warwickshire is still a thatched
      county

By gift and purchase the Trust has amassed a rich collection of Shakespeariana, and one of the finest manuscript collections in Britain—borough archives since medieval times on Warwickshire generally and Stratford in particular. This includes the only known surviving letter written to Shakespeare, in which Richard Quyney, whose son Thomas married the poet's daughter Judith, requests a loan of £30. The library and records are available to accredited students.

Quite independent and self-governing, the Trust receives no grant from state or local authorities, and depends entirely on admission fees and a few investments. Library, administrative, and clerical staff, guide lecturers and receptionists at the properties, gardeners, and general staff number approximately 100 in winter and 150 in summer. In 1950 the number of visitors to the birthplace was 136,193. By 1969 the figure had risen to 390,704, and a recent five-year period revealed 130 different overseas countries of origin of signatories of the visitors' books.

Opinions on Stratford may vary with the visitor's interests, but in one particular the town is superlative—the attraction of its inn signs. The 'Oddfellows', Windsor Street, has two of the Bard's odd fellows on either side of its sign, Bottom with Falstaff, and Shylock with a clown, possibly Touchstone, and for another wholly Shakespearian sign we go to the 'Three Witches' on the Alcester road at Shottery. In Shottery, too, is the cottage where Shakespeare came courting Anne Hathaway, of all the shrines perhaps the most felicitous, set in an English garden, tree embowered, with a capacious car park far enough away not to be intrusive. Groups of schoolchildren, multi-lingual crowds some in colourful costume, often an artist selling his sketches on the spot, and, a few steps away, the heather garden in front of the home of one of our Czech allies who has returned to live in the Warwickshire where he was once stationed in wartime.

Back in Stratford, intended as a reference to *Henry V* or no, the 'White Swan', ducally gorged and chained on the sign of the hotel, was the badge of that monarch so prominent in the plays. On the Evesham Road, the 'Salmon's Tail' probably gets its unique name from a fifteenth-century enclosure so called thereabouts, though Iago did say of Desdemona, 'She that in wisdom never was so frail,

To change a cod's head for the salmon's tail.' The 'Globe' is not the reference it seems to the London theatre; its sign depicts a wizard gazing into a crystal ball. The 'Garrick' in High Street, however, is all it seems, with a painting of the great Shakespearian actor looking up from its sign on the inn's restored Elizabethan façade, at the statue of Shakespeare on the Town Hall, which the actor presented in his jubilee year, 1769. American visitors are attracted to the Red Horse Hotel in Bridge Street where Washington Irving wrote his account of Stratford in his famous *Sketch Book*.

Shakespeare's family crest accounts for the name of the Falcon Hotel, while the 'Windmill', with the oldest unbroken licence in the town, claims that Shakespeare possibly drank there, and designates its toilets 'Romeos' and 'Juliets'. The thirteenth-century grammar school and the almshouses, between the Guild Chapel and the 'Windmill' in Church Street, provide one of Stratford's most beautiful groups. There is no more colourful sign in the town than that of the 'George', Bridge Street, with the Prince Regent's head against the turrets of Brighton Pavilion. In Ely Street the familiar 'Cross Keys' has a white glove across the intersection of the keys and a white rose in each handle—why? Almost opposite, the 'Queen's Head' sign portrays Catherine Howard on one side and Elizabeth of York on the other. The 'Sportsman' sign in Bull Street blazons an athletic individual strangely accoutred for and beset by the implements of so many games that he reminds me of Bottom, anxious to play every part in 'Pyramus and Thisbe.'

The Old Tramway Inn, already mentioned, is joined by another transport name and sign at the 'Anchor' on Waterside, a reminder that from 1650 to 1800 vessels up to 40 tons gave Stratford 'the appearance of a small seaport town' according to William Smith, for, encouraged by Charles I, William Sandys of Fladbury, downstream in Worcestershire, was aiming to make the Avon navigable from Tewkesbury to Coventry. The Civil War curtailed his efforts, but over the past 20 years or so the Lower Avon Navigation Trust has been trying to emulate him, and in 1971 earned considerable disapprobation from the unsightly lock it erected above the weir.

Most famous of Stratford hostelries is surely the 'Black Swan', hard by the theatre and the resort of many famous actors sometimes to be seen sitting on the terrace. Few pubs can have become

43

so popular under their nickname that they must be listed by it in the telephone directory, but you will find this establishment under both 'Black Swan' and 'Dirty Duck', while the latter now occupies one side of the sign.

Residents of Stratford pay less apparent heed to Shakespeare than might be expected. Recently I made a fairly careful check of house names in the town and found three only with Shakespearean associations—'Portia', 'Verona', and Cymbeline House, while one wool shop was called the 'Merrie Wives'. The one occasion beside the Mop Fair in October which brings all Stratfordians into Bridge Street, so spacious because it had a line of small houses, Middle Row, in the centre until the mid-nineteenth century—is the Birthday Celebration, when the flags of many countries are unfurled and civic and visiting notables process to Holy Trinity Church.

Shakespeare died on his birthday, 23 April 1616, and his remains lie in the chancel of Holy Trinity beneath a monument by Gerard Johnson, known to have been in position in 1623. On his stone is the doggerel:

> *Good frend for Jesus' sake forbeare,*
> *To digg the dust encloased heare:*
> *Blest be ye man yt spares thes stones,*
> *And curst be he yt moves my bones.*

Beside Shakespeare lie his wife, Susanna, his favourite child, with Dr. Hall her husband, and Thomas Nash, husband to Shakespeare's granddaughter Elizabeth. The registers with the entries of the poet's baptism and burial are on display, and the fifteenth-century font is the one in which he was baptized. An 'American Window' in the chancel depicts the Seven Ages of Man from *As You Like It* in Old Testament characters. The great 'American Window' in the south wall includes Archbishop Laud, who first suggested sending a bishop to America; Seabury, first Bishop of Connecticut; Amerigo Vespucci, Christopher Columbus, William Penn, and St. Eric, first Bishop of Greenland. The 'Preachers' Window' in the north wall, includes an exceptionally fine portrait of Savonarola, and the 'Physicians' Window' the rare twin saints Cosmas, with a pestle and mortar, and Damien, with a retort.

The carving in the choir stalls should not be missed, though many faces have been hacked from the misericords beneath the hinged seats. Some of these depict violent discord between the sexes —a wife beating her husband who is upside down and being bitten by a dog; a woman clutching a man by his beard as she beats him with a saucepan, and another lady, even less considerate, who is kicking a knight in his private parts. And a certain irreverent monkey must not be missed.

Sir Hugh Clopton, the bridge builder, directed in his will that should he die at Stratford he be buried in the Clopton Chapel, formerly the Lady Chapel. Dying in London, however, he was buried there, but the Clopton Chapel holds, nevertheless, a wealth of interest. The south transept has Holy Trinity's outstanding epitaph —in Hebrew, Greek, Latin, and English—a portion of which tells us:

> *Here lieth intombed the corps of Richarde Hill*
> *A woollen draper being in his time:*
> *Whose virtues live, whose fame dooth flourish still*
> *Though hee desolved be to dust and slime*

Clopton House, still much as Shakespeare knew it, stands in parkland a mile north of Stratford. The Manor of Clopton gave its name to the family of one Robert, a substantial yeoman into whose possession it came in the thirteenth century. Clopton House itself dates from the sixteenth century, was enlarged by Sir John Clopton around 1670 and remodelled in the eighteenth century. Its most illustrious occupant was, of course, Sir Hugh Clopton, the wealthy mercer who became Lord Mayor of London in the reign of Henry VII. In addition to building the bridge of 14 arches he restored the Guild Chapel and built New Place. It is supposed that at Clopton House Shakespeare laid Scene II from the Introduction to *The Taming of the Shrew*, in which Christopher Sly, having gone to sleep a drunken tinker outside an alehouse, awakes richly apparelled in 'a bedchamber in the Lord's House'.

Clopton House is the home of Lady Utica Beecham, who, one December day when a fierce gale was raging, accompanied me along the gallery to the foot of a steep wooden staircase. There she left me alone to explore the attic where a priest was murdered in the sixteenth century and his body thrown into the moat, leaving—so they say—his ghost to haunt the upper rooms at Clopton.

The landing above the staircase was low-ceilinged and gloomy, and a piercing whistle beneath the door of the murder room changed as I opened it to the crescendo of a savage elemental onslaught as a prolonged gust shook the dormers and roared in the chimneys. I spoke aloud the line from *Othello*—'A fuller blast ne'er shook our battlements'. In the room a shadow moved over the floor and along a wall—cast from windborne clouds scurrying across the sun. As the gust spent itself among the roaring elms where the lawns gave way to parkland, the hangings on the old-fashioned bed stirred uneasily, and, on the floor at its foot, were the three marks said to be the bloodstains of the murdered priest.

It was a fitting dramatic spot to recall that items in the history of the Cloptons bear striking resemblance to situations in Shakespeare's plays. In the Oak Room at Clopton there is a window with the arms of many generations of Cloptons and their wives. One shield which bears the same device for both husband and wife is dated 1595, in which year a couple of Clopton cousins were married at Holy Trinity, aged 12 and 15. This juvenile romance could have inspired the tragedy of the young star-crossed lovers *Romeo and Juliet*, published in 1597. In the year of Shakespeare's birth, 1564, some joy came to the Cloptons in the birth of a daughter, Margaret, but great sorrow came also, as it did to many in Stratford that year, for plague ravaged the town, among the victims being Charlotte Clopton. Quick burial was essential, so Charlotte's body was hurried to the vault in the Clopton Chapel. Several days afterwards the vault was opened for some reason, disclosing a scene of horror. Charlotte was standing at the doorway, dead. One of her shoulders was badly bitten, presumably by the girl herself in anguish at waking to find herself entombed.

Though this happened just as Shakespeare was born the gruesome story lived on, and could well have been in Shakespeare's mind when he brought Juliet to life in her tomb to find the bodies of Romeo and Paris beside her. Margaret Clopton, too, came to an untimely end probably providing Ophelia's death scene in *Hamlet*. Looking from a dormer across the wind-wracked grounds of Clopton towards the fishpond with its tangle of brambles and briers and the tossing elm branches overhead, I recalled Queen Gertrude's words:

> *One woe doth tread upon another's heel,*
> *So fast they follow. Your sister's drowned, Laertes.*

For here, sick for love, Margaret Clopton drowned herself, to become the prototype of the mad Ophelia. For a while I gazed on the sinister pool. Sheltered though it is the gale penetrated its defences, sending cats'paws to disturb the dark surface, until it seemed that the ghost of the lovelorn Margaret was about to rise from the depths to join the priest's ghost in the attics of Clopton House.

Across the attic landing is St. Peter's Chapel, or the 'text room' as it is known from several texts painted on the walls, one within a heart shape. A simple altar and four bulky prie-dieus are all the furnishing in this room which reminds me, in its austerity, of the chamber at Berkeley Castle where Edward ii was murdered.

Eastward of Clopton House, like a rocket poised for launching, the 120-ft. Welcombe obelisk points to the skies just outside Stratford on the way to Snitterfield—a familiar landmark, though few know who or what it commemorates. In 1816 the Manor of Snitterfield was sold by George, Earl of Coventry, for £65,000 to Robert Philips, a Manchester cotton manufacturer who, like many of his kind, were seeking dignified houses in the desirable Midlands countryside. The new squire, however, soon demolished the Stuart manor house beside the church and used the stone to enlarge Park House, Snitterfield, which on Robert's death in 1844 became the home of his son, Mark. It was Mark Philips in whose honour the Welcombe obelisk was built in 1876 by his younger brother, Robert Needham Philips. Mark's accomplishments and virtues are recorded on the plinth.

When the Great Reform Act gave Manchester Parliamentary representation in 1832, Mark was its first M.P., and for 15 years as a Liberal he took particular interest in education and civil and religious liberty. He was a staunch opponent of those 'taxes upon knowledge'—the stamp duty, the advertisement duty, and the newspaper duty. Mark was something of a pioneer left-winger, upholding working-class rights and sympathizing with the French Revolution. In 1830 he travelled to Paris to congratulate the French people on the success of the revolution. The eulogy on the obelisk refers to his 'rare flow of wit and humour' and he was of genial mien and portly frame.

Another face of the plinth pays tribute to Robert Philips, the father, who raised a petition against the war with America and was nearly mobbed in Manchester. In 1830 he declined a baronetcy proffered by the Whigs. Nor is the builder of the obelisk forgotten, a testimony to him having been added posthumously. Robert Needham Philips died in 1890, having followed the family trade as a cotton manufacturer, and was M.P. for Bury for 22 years.

For all the obelisk's prominence, standing there on its hill, the locality has two other Philips monuments—the village of Snitterfield, to which they contributed so much, and the many-chimneyed, Jacobean-gabled pile of the Welcombe Hotel, set so beautifully in its grounds below the obelisk, the essence of Warwickshire at its leafiest and loveliest. There is no more charming approach to any building in the Midlands than that serpentine half-mile drive, paved with the saffron and gold of autumn trees, with squirrels bounding about the green banks on either hand. The Welcombe has lost nothing in its change from stately home to luxury hotel.

In 1845 Mark Philips bought Welcombe Lodge from Charles Thomas Warde—a house rebuilt in 1815 by George Lloyd. It did not long endure under Mark's ownership; by 1869 he had erected in its place the present mansion. At his death, unmarried, in 1871, he was succeeded by his brother, who in turn left the entire estate to his daughter, Caroline, who, in the same year that Welcombe was built, had married George Otto Trevelyan, writer and statesman, despite opposition from Uncle Mark. When her husband inherited his family baronetcy Caroline became Lady Trevelyan, and it was their son who sold Welcombe House and its grounds to Sir Archibald Flower, the Stratford brewer. In 1931 the L.M.S. Railway Company acquired the mansion as a hotel.

There is little evidence of the Philipses at the 'Welcombe' today, though the lounge has a fine fireplace bearing the family's crest, a lion holding a lozenge enclosing a fleur-de-lys. Among guests at the

'Welcombe' none is better remembered than the late King Farouk of Egypt, who used handkerchiefs with an 'F' monogram which he discarded after a single use. Krishna Menon stayed there; so too Malik as Russian Ambassador, while Chinese Communist delegations to various Shakespeare festivals have enjoyed high living in 'Welcombe's' luxury.

In Snitterfield memories of the Philips family die hard. Among their tablets in the church one tells how a poignant tragedy befell this family on which fortune otherwise shone so brightly. On 2 November 1824, Jessy Ann Philips, sister of Mark and Robert Needham, died at Malvern, aged 16, just six months after the death of her twin, Elizabeth Lucy. The popularity of the Philipses and the Trevelyans survived what might have been bad beginnings. Robert Philips closed four of Snitterfield's five inns. Then Lady Trevelyan signalized her inheritance by closing the Bell Brook Inn in the village, and one other on the Stratford-Warwick road. Maybe some resentment is shown to the closure of the Bell Brook Inn, for the 'History Scrapbook', compiled by Snitterfield Women's Institute, recalls astonishing hauntings at Brook House, as the old inn is now called.

The tenants during the Second World War several times saw 'a big black dog which ran over the soft earth in the garden seed beds leaving no footmarks'. One evening as they sat in the former bar-parlour they watched 'a large oval ectoplasm develop and hover round for an hour'.

Snitterfield Church, once in Worcester diocese, has in its east window four Bishops of Worcester who were canonized—Egwin, Oswald, Dunstan, and Wulstan. Buried in the churchyard, the exact spot unknown, is Shakespeare's uncle Henry. This charming village narrowly missed great fame, for Robert Shakespeare, grandfather of the poet, settled there in 1535 as a small farmer, and John, father of William, was born there, moving to Stratford in 1551.

Nowhere in the Midlands is a war memorial so pleasantly sited as at Snitterfield—a tall cross on the bluff of White Horse Hill, with a stone seat commanding a breathtaking panorama of the Avon valley, a place to dream away a summer's day. The seat is dedicated to Lady Trevelyan—Caroline Philips—and the inscription was chosen by Sir George: 'The noble expanse visible from this spot was Shakespeare's favourite countryside. The men whose names are inscribed on the neighbouring monument gave their lives for that England "Which never did, and never shall, lie at the proud foot of a conqueror."'

CHAPTER THREE

The Shakespeare
Villages and Alcester

One of the few stories told about Shakespeare concerns a famous drinking bout at Bidford-on-Avon, seven miles by road and nine winding miles downstream from Stratford. He had gone with some bibulous cronies to take on the Bidford Topers in a drinking contest one Whit Monday, but the Topers had already departed for Evesham Fair. Bidford, however had a second team, the Sippers, who promptly drank the visitors under the table at the Falcon. Beating an uncertain retreat, the Stratfordians staggered barely a mile homewards before resting underneath a crab tree where they fell asleep and stayed the night. Waking with a hangover, Shakespeare vowed never again to drink with the men of

> Piping Pebworth, dancing Marston,
> Haunted Hillborough, hungry Grafton,
> Dodging Exhall, Papist Wixford,
> Beggerly Broom and drunken Bidford.

These villages were all visible from Shakespeare's Crab, as it became known. It was removed in a decayed state to Bidford Grange on 1 December 1824, and its position is not marked today.

Pebworth is in Worcestershire, the other seven in Warwickshire, and with another half-dozen villages omitted from Shakespeare's doggerel, they comprise a motoring itinerary around a landscape as gracious as it is spacious, with views bounded only by the Cotswold Edge, Bredon Hill, and the Malvern Hills. It is a fruitful countryside, the flood plain of the Avon providing fertile chocolate soil for the Horticultural Experimental Station at Luddington, while farther westward its orchards and brassica fields merge with the regimented husbandry of Worcestershire in the Vale of Evesham.

Leaving Stratford by the Evesham road we come within four miles to a right turn for Binton, where St. Peter's Church still has mounting steps and a tethering ring for horse-borne parishioners. Here from 1906 to 1924 the Rev. Lloyd Hervey Bruce was rector, and his humble memorial, down the steps near the church door, is overshadowed by the more famous memorial west window. The sister of the rector, Kathleen, married Captain Robert Falcon Scott, and together they often visited the recory, the last time being shortly before Scott sailed in the *Terra Nova* in 1910 for his last journey to the Antarctic. There he reached the South Pole on 17 January 1912, but died on the return journey with his four companions.

On 25 September 1915 a memorial window to these intrepid explorers was unveiled at Binton by the Duke of Newcastle. The tiny wheatsheaf enclosing something like a black chess rook in the bottom left corner stamps the window as the work of Kempe and Tower, and it has four roundels depicting the Polar quintet bidding farewell to the last supporting party, the discovery of the flag that showed Amundsen had beaten them to the Pole by a month, Oates sacrificing himself in the blizzard, and the cairn erected over the bodies of Scott, Wilson and Bowers by the search party.

The crowded visitors' book at Binton was begun in April 1964 during the celebration of the 400th anniversary of the birth of Shakespeare. On Boxing Day 1964 it was signed by a young man who came there from his father's home at Welford, just across the Avon. He was Wally Herbert who, in 1968-69, led a party afoot from Point Barrow, Alaska, to Spitzbergen across the North Pole. Lady Scott—as the explorer's widow was created—was a considerable sculptress, and her rector brother's memorial is a small wooden crucifix with a young beardless Christ in bronze which she fashioned.

Scott shares the interest at Binton with Sir John Greville, who sat in five parliaments and died in 1480. His arms appear in a window, saved in the original glass from a window in an earlier church. A plaque explains that he is buried at Weston-super-Avon —to our generations Weston-on-Avon, two miles away.

At the first crossroads, a mile north-east of Binton, the Blue Boar Inn flaunts its sign dwarfed by a magnificent elm. Have you ever wondered why the boars of pub signs are always blue—never pink, purple, or spotted? They hark back to days when sycophantic landlords named their taverns after the white boar badge of Richard

III. With his defeat and death at Bosworth in 1485 they felt somewhat exposed to the victorious Lancastrian, Henry VII, until one of them realized that the Lancastrian Earl of Oxford had a blue boar as his badge. So out came their ladders, and up they went to paint their white boars blue.

We have risen steadily from the Avon valley, and a switchback mile from the Blue Boar brings us to our first of the 'jingle' villages, Temple Grafton—'hungry' Grafton because of its poor stony soil on a hilltop site. Its church, with a broach spire, dedicated to St. Andrew, was rebuilt in 1875. Its Saxon predecessor is one of several churches believed to have been the venue of Shakespeare's marriage, which took place in November 1582. A licence was granted by the Bishop of Worcester for the poet's marriage to Anne Whateley of Temple Grafton, not Anne Hathaway of Shottery. Some see a similarity to Hathaway in the surname of Shakespeare's 'other Anne', but Temple Grafton can hardly be confused with Shottery.

A century ago one Charles Green published an account of his walk round the eight Shakespeare villages. Between Bidford and Temple Grafton he wrote of two miles amid 'the hateful reek of limekilns', for lime was quarried in the blue lias. Of 29 workers in Grafton in 1854, ten were quarrymen or stonemasons, and there is still evidence of the old quarries southward from the 'hungry' village.

The road to 'Dodging Exhall' takes in charming little Arden's Grafton with its lilliputian cottages, and Little Britain embowered in orchards. 'Dodging', 'dadging', or 'dudgeon' Exhall—this is the least comprehensible of Shakespeare's epithets, but the peace and beauty of its colourful gardens have not many visitors from Birmingham and Coventry contemplating retirement. Here Mrs. Fanny Reeves was born, and here, taking over from her mother at 19, she was verger for 55 years until they laid her to rest in her own churchyard in 1965. Still her husband rings the church bell, keeping up the continuity so characteristic of village life. For over 50 years Bill Reeves was cowman at Exhall Court Farm. My sojourn was shorter—just a week in November 1940 with my comrades of 428 (Shirley) Searchlight Battery, R.A., in action during the blitzes on Birmingham and Coventry. We each had a personal corn-bin high up in the mill, sweet-smelling quarters with a modicum of privacy, from which, on a 'Take Post' we descended fireman-like down a stout rope through several floors.

There is some justification for calling Wixford 'Papist', for the influence of the Throckmortons of Coughton Court was strong there. They were, and are, a leading Roman Catholic family. For long they kept up the Chapel of St. John in the otherwise reformed church dedicated to St. Milburgh. In pre-Reformation times the Canons of Kenilworth had to pay 46s. per annum towards the upkeep of the chapel, and to see that Mass was said there three days a week. In 1669 six villagers petitioned the bishop to restrain the incumbent of Wixford, the Rev. Mr. Kecke, from felling a venerable yew in the churchyard. Mr. Kecke told the bishop that this was 'false information from Papistical parishioners'—so the word has for long been bandied about there.

The yew still stands, supported by many crutches, and has, as neighbour, the thatched shed where visiting preachers stabled their horses. St. Milburgh, an abbess with a lamb at her feet, shares the east window with St. Christopher. A brass on the tomb of Thomas Crewe and his wife is an outstanding example of fifteenth-century craftsmanship. Though attorney to the Countess of Warwick he is portrayed in full armour, and mystery is given to the brass by a human foot repeated several times.

Wixford is famous for its fishing in the River Arrow, so the name of the riverside inn, the 'Fish', needs no explanation. Its other inn, the 'Three Horse Shoes', is an attractive place, festooned in wistaria, with two walnut trees on the forecourt. Why three horse shoes rather than four? The answer is that pubs so named stood next to smithies, the horseman consoling himself with ale while the blacksmith replaced a cast shoe on his mount. Certainly a smithy once stood beside the 'Three Horse Shoes' at Wixford.

'Beggarly' Broom seems a gross calumny on a village situated in a veritable cornucopia of orchards, soft fruits, and fields of cabbage, sprouts, broccoli, and cauliflowers. A mill on the Arrow, which has been in the Edkins family for more than a century, gives an added air of prosperity to the village, while Broom Hall Country Club, hiding much of its magpie beauty behind a fine holm oak, has had a considerable facelift since its 20 odd years as a youth hostel. It was 1577, the year when Drake started his voyage round the world, that Sir Thomas Throckmorton began building this timber-framed hall. In one respect Broom has lost out to progress—its station, Broom Junction, was closed around 1960 after passenger services to Stratford had ceased on 16 June 1947. This line had come to Broom from Stratford Old Town Station on 2 June 1879 to join the Evesham and Redditch line. It was 46 miles long, originating at Blisworth, Northamptonshire, on the London and North Western line. Called the Stratford and Midland Junction Railway, its initials, the S.M.J., lent themselves to the irreverence of wags. The Slow Mournful Journey was a frequent play on them; the Slow Man's Joy, and the Stratford Monkey Jumper. Even a former Lord Willoughby de Broke contributed his quip: 'There is nothing vulgar about the S.M.J.—like indecent haste.' He was on the board, and one summer Sunday he entertained the entire staff at his home, Compton Verney.

During its passenger life the S.M.J. made two interesting innovations. On 20 April 1911 it introduced the 'Railophone', giving telephone communication between the train and a fixed point, with the Mayor of Stratford in the train and Marie Corelli the novelist, in Stratford. The novelty was short-lived, but was developed as a train-control device. Then in 1932, in L.M.S. days, came the 'Ro-railer', a single-deck motor bus with separate steel-flanged rubber-tyred wheels which enabled it to travel the metals from Blisworth and change to the road at Old Town Station, from where it continued to the railway's Welcombe Hotel.

Broom Junction would have been a delightful place to change trains on a late summer's morning. with a tawny cornfield coming up to its western boundary and Broom Mill rising from the willow-shaded Arrow to eastward. Two old stagers from Broom Junction were still alive with their memories in October 1970, Edwin Gould, signalman, aged 95, and Alfred Edge, stationmaster. Among Mr. Edge's memories were special hunt trains passing through for Alcester from the Warwickshire Hunt kennels at Kineton, and, each August, a special train also from Kineton, in which a wealthy landowner took his family, friends, and staff, to the grouse-shooting in Scotland.

At 'Drunken' Bidford, the next station from Broom, George Mayrick once reminisced to me of his days as leading porter before the Second World War.

'In spring,' he said, 'we would load six trucks of cabbages from Bickmarsh Farm by 8 a.m. Mr. Fred Holder would bring us about four truckloads of garden produce each day—it went mostly to Birmingham stations or the Potteries. We'd have ten loads of hay weekly for Manchester and for firms in Birmingham. In the season there would be 20 trucks of fruit daily, often for a jam factory, and Stratford had to send us a mid-day engine to clear the one siding we had. Then in winter, there'd be sprouts and savoys. Gill's brickyard beside the station brought in their coal and sent out their bricks by rail.'

In the Warwickshire volume of his 'Buildings of England' series, Sir Nikolaus Pevsner says of Bidford: 'The main street is that of a little town, not a village. The houses line the street with few breaks.' One of these breaks leads to the parish church, which has a window to its patronal saint, Lawrence, standing on the gridiron of his martyrdom. 'The Falcon', of Shakespeare's toping downfall, is still there on Church Street corner, mullioned and transomed, no longer an inn but a private residence, having had one spell as a workhouse. Another break in that main street, beside the 'White Lion', leads to the eight-arched bridge across the Avon, a narrow fifteenth-century structure with cutwaters which continues to hold its own against twentieth-century traffic which is unable to pass on the bridge.

Crossing early one morning I spoke very sharply to a woman driver who disputed my passage when obviously I had right of way. I drove a couple of miles down the Roman Buckle Street, pulled up, and looked around for a possible place to dump my car while I went for a day's walk. A woman in a cottage asked if I was lost, and hearing what I sought, kindly told me to drive into the empty one of two garages beside her cottage. I said I would return around 5.30 p.m., and spent the day walking on the Cotswold Edge. When I arrived back she had tea laid for three and invited me to sit down, saying her friend would be home any moment. Almost immediately a car stopped outside, the door opened, and there was the lady I had slanged on the bridge nine hours earlier.

It pays to take a basket along this road south of the Avon, for there are bargains to be had in fruit and vegetables as you pass through Barton, with its 'Cottage of Content Inn'. A thatched roof

11 *Coughton Court, near Alcester, home of the Throckmorton family*

12 *The magnificent entrance hall at Ragley Hall, home of the Marquess of Hertford*

near the inn is 'signed' with the straw weathercock of the Cresswell family of Offenham, near Evesham, thatchers for centuries, whose work, similarly signed, can be seen also at Sambourne, Wilmcote, and Lower Quinton.

Southernmost of the Warwickshire 'jingle' villages, 'Dancing' Marston, or Long Marston has associations with one of Britain's best-known historic journeys. Beside Manor Farm, another drive curves round a dark willow-fringed pool and a massive elm to King's Lodge, where the original grey stone outcrops from more recent brick. Here, on his clandestine journey south after the royal oak incident at Boscobel, Charles II is said to have emulated one of his predecessors, King Alfred, in proving an incompetent cook. Charles was travelling as Will Jackson, servant to Jane Lane, and when they made an overnight stop at Long Marston with the loyalist Tomes family, Jackson was sent to help in the kitchen, where he was deputed to turn the spit for the roast. His fumbling earned the disapprobation of the cook, shown by a buffet about the royal ears, though it is probably fabrication that Roundhead searchers called in time to laugh at the assault.

Long Marston Church repays closer than a cursory glance. The stormlight of a boisterous October afternoon was on its yellow walls and grey shingles when last I saw it, and the churchyard was redolent with a cider-smell from an orchard across the road bowed down with apples and pears. Acceptable enough from outside, the saddleback tower is a revelation inside the church, supported on giant beams, themselves anchored on others lying horizontal. Most of the memorials are to the Tomes, one of whom, Captain Geoffrey Tomes of the 53rd Sikhs, lies where he fell at Gallipoli. Here too is that most Warwickshire of surnames—the rose bushes in the church-yard are in memory of Richard and Bessie Arden. Once known as Dry Marston or Marston Sicca, which means the same thing, the village deserves its appellation of 'Dancing' Marston, for in the words of Charles Green over a century ago: 'In this village there existed, time out of mind, a band of morris-dancers who were wont to attend the wakes, fairs, and merry meetings for many miles around. Fantastically decked with ribbons, with bells attached to their legs, they were accompanied by a tabor and piper who, with a "Motley fool", were a source of great amusement to their rustic neighbours.'

13   *Alcester*

Northward of Long Marston, Welford and Weston spread neighbourly together 'on Avon'. The latter should not be neglected, having a satisfying church of great congruity, and one cul-de-sac of thatched cottage delight to rival the famous Boat Lane of its neighbour. Welford's 'Four Alls'—unhappily without any sign—and its slender red, white, and blue maypole with a fox windvane, are well known.

Welford Church has much the same history as Little Compton Church (Chapter 1). in 1059, Sweyn, Earl of Gloucester, gave Welford to the Saxon priory of Deerhurst, which was a cell of the Abbey of St. Denis in Paris. The monks of Deerhurst built a church on the present site at Welford, soon to be replaced by the Norman edifice of which so much remains, particularly the arcades. With the Hundred Years War, Welford was taken from the alien house of Deerhurst and given to the Abbot of Tewkesbury, but the old association is recorded in a recent east window by Christopher Webb, which includes St. Denis—as Dionysius—holding the French fleur-de-lys. Another rare French saint is there, St. Yves or Ivo of Brittany—patron of lawyers.

Until recently Welford Church boasted probably the oldest lychgate in England. Becoming unsafe, it has been replaced, and though it is a careful replica, its newness is apparent. Beyond the church a placid and fairly wide reach of the Avon flows towards the old mill weir. From the Bidford road, a mile out of Welford, there is as near a bird's-eye view of the Avon as one gets, where the road climbs high close above the river. On the far, northern, bank is 'Haunted' Hillborough, a rambling farmhouse dating back to Stephen's reign. Remote, down a dead-end lane, it certainly looks a likely place for a haunting, and a previous occupant told me that the ghost is that of Shakespeare's 'other Anne'—the mysterious Anne Whateley. Black and white timbering mingles with the cream-coloured limestone of Hillborough. Indoors it has some splendid panelling, and the corridors between its bedrooms and the lofty attic make a wonderful spot for a ghost. The circular dovecote is as exciting as the house. From a central brick pillar, eight radial beams support a platform in the dome, and in the walls are 1,000 pigeon-holes.

There is supposedly another haunting at Cranhill Corner on the

A439 only half a mile from the Hillborough lane. Mr. Clarence Bailey of Cranhill Farm told me the story.

'There was once a gibbet on this corner', he said, 'and on it they hanged Palmer the Poisoner. It is his ghost which is supposed to haunt the area.'

I protested that Palmer did his poisoning at Rugeley in Staffordshire and was hanged at Stafford, but suggested that perhaps because of his notoriety any lesser poisoner was called Palmer. Mr. Bailey, however, thought this one was named Palmer and that he poisoned his wife at Welford. Then he played his trump card.

'In any case', he said, 'that field of mine opposite Cranhill Corner has always been known as Palmer's Piece.'

North of the Stratford-Alcester road, today the A422, but once a track trodden by the Roman legions, a pleasant 12-mile walk takes in a number of Shakespeare shrines. Leaving Stratford by the canal towpath, a mile brings the walker to the Royal Victoria Spa at Bishopton. Medicinal wells had been sunk, but not even the patronage of the Princess Victoria raised the venture to rivalry with Leamington Spa to which it aspired. Today the spa building is called Bruce Lodge after a resident to whom the First World War brought lustre comparable to that of many a general. An electrician at the Stratford Memorial Theatre, he became Captain Bruce Bairnsfather, the famous war artist, creator of Old Bill and his Better 'Ole, the walrus-moustached private soldier, compounded, so Captain Bairnsfather once told me, of a number of military characters.

In 1964 Queen Elizabeth, the Queen Mother, opened the 12 miles of the southern end of the Stratford Canal, restored by the National Trust, who are now its custodians. Beyond the Royal Victoria Spa, in the vicinity of Lock 41, inscriptions on bollards and locks record gifts towards the restoration of this charming waterway, and near the bridge at Wilmcote, three miles along the canal from Stratford, stands Mary Arden's House, the girlhood home of Shakespeare's mother. A beautiful half-timbered small farmhouse, now a museum of country crafts and tools, with a fine dovecote, it is, to my mind, the most attractive of the Shakespeare shrines.

Mary Arden would have gone to her wedding at Aston Cantlow by much the same three miles of lane that we walk today, past the occasional cottage of cream-blue lias, the limestone rock from an old quarry at Newnham, behind the tree line of the Rough Hills. Here, in July, are found the limestone flowers, yellow centaury and bee orchid among them, with the autumn gentian or felwort coming later. Around 1600 the quarrying of this felicitous building stone began at Temple Grafton, moving later to Newnham, thence to Ettington, and finally to Harbury.

Aston Cantlow Church has an additional distinction to that momentous marriage between John Shakespeare and Mary Arden. It is the only Warwickshire church to have had an incumbent who became a saint. This was Thomas de Cantelupe, who appears as a bishop in an east window by Kempe. St. Thomas became Bishop of Hereford in 1275 and Chancellor of England. But to visitors, Aston Cantlow means most often the King's Head, where the name of Edkins is synonymous with 'duck suppers'. The villagers themselves look perhaps with most pride on the black and white Guildhall, which was restored by local effort and is used as a village hall.

The River Alne meanders willow-fringed from Aston Cantlow to Great Alne, and bramble and willow-herb steadily obliterate the old Alcester Railway, opened in 1876 from a junction with the North Warwickshire line at Bearley to connect Stratford-upon-Avon with Alcester, but long since abandoned. At Haselor Grounds the river glides down a weir while a mill stream continues to Great Alne Mill which still lifts its flour-whitened cowls above the meadows though milling ceased a decade or more ago. To the mill has come more recently, as resident, Mr. Derek Ogden, a former electrical engineer, who in his middle thirties decided to set up as a millwright, and has worked on the renovation of a number of England's remaining windmills and water mills.

Great Alne's erstwhile railway station, though converted into a residence and the local post office, still bears such striking marks of its original function as to mystify the stranger in the complete absence of a railway line. More mystery is generated by the name of the Mother Huff Cap Inn, a picturesque 'museum' of superannuated wagons and wagon wheels. The inn sign gives a clue to the name —a buxom barmaid holding a foaming tankard. The 'huff cap' is the froth head on a glass of ale.

Beside the inn the Philomela Café is a well-known haunt of

ramblers coming in by field track from the Alne Hills along the footpath from the church. Memorial seats are becoming more frequent today, one in Great Alne churchyard inscribed 'Rest Awhile' being in memory of Paul Martin Simcox, who died in June 1968, aged only 18. Many Americans touring the Shakespeare country pass through this churchyard. One came to stay, at rest beneath a small white stone which tells us that he is 'Thomas Edison. U.S. Air Force, World War Two, September 22, 1905; July 1, 1961'.

Industry has come to Great Alne with the Maudsley Works. The factory is hidden from the winding road, but some widening of this has taken away the old cricket pavilion which was another of my wartime searchlight billets when the Germans dropped several delayed-action bombs around our equipment, sending us temporarily into more congenial lodgings down the road at the Boot Inn, now no more.

A mile along the Alcester road from Alne End, Kinwarton's tiny church nestles beside the gracious Georgian red brick of the former rectory, while through a field gate is a fourteenth-century dovecote. Now in the care of the National Trust, this circular grey stone structure has more than 500 nesting holes in its interior walls, still accessible by a well-preserved potence—the ladder on an arm which protrudes from a rotating central pole. Kinwarton Church has borrowed from neighbouring Worcestershire that favourite name-saint, Richard of Droitwich, depicted as Bishop of Chichester in a memorial window to Canon Richard Seymour, 42 years rector, who died in 1880.

A short meadow path from Kinwarton runs beside an exquisite stretch of the Alne, bright with yellow brandy-bottle water lilies, to Hoo Mill. The river is on its last mile to a confluence with the Arrow at Alcester, and in Hoo Mill it has a charming conversion near its end, as it has near its beginning in Mill House, Danzey. In 1844 a Redditch needle manufacturer, Holyoake, added a needle mill to the existing grist mill at Hoo, with a lease 'for three lives'. The Stewart family had already been in residence there for four years, and there they remained until, on his marriage in 1919, Arthur Crampton Stewart bought the entire property. After a stoppage he repaired the mill wheel with the help of J. Hilson and Sons of Langley, Warwickshire, and had it turning again to celebrate

'V.J.' Day. An inscription on the wheel giving this information is read through an internal window in a fascinating room built by Mr. Stewart in place of the needle mill. This large window looks on to the ponderous mill wheel, while across the room the external window is misted with spray from the weir beside it. Between the windows the floor is paved—of all things—with wooden broomheads, And like Kipling's mill in 'Puck's Song', Hoo Mill was mentioned in Domesday Book:

> *See you our little mill that clacks,*
> *So busy by the brook?*
> *She has ground her corn and paid her tax*
> *Ever since Domesday Book.*

It is little more than a mile's walk eastward from Hoo Mill to Haselor Church, which never fails to remind me of Goldsmith's 'decent church that topt the neighbouring hill'. A tarmac footpath leads up to the church from the still-preserved stocks at Upton, and descends, round the east end beneath massive elms and passing the base of an ancient cross, to the charming hamlet of Walcot, where a cider mill has been reconstructed by the Finnemore family in a garden fully in view of the passer-by. Paul Pry Cottage nearby perpetuates the name of a onetime inn.

Pied flycatchers always sport around Haselor's tree-fringed churchyard in early summer, and snug in an alcove beneath the Norman tower is another memorial seat, to 'N. Morris, September 1953'. Lit by a westering sun this is a splendid place to soak in the essential hedgerow glory of a widespread Warwickshire landscape. Among those of my walking friends who have shared that seat with me is one who is now remembered in a memorial seat of his own. True, it is a mile across the Worcestershire border on the western slope of the Lickey Hills, near Birmingham, but Alderman Jack Wood, who died in 1969, aged 72, was one of Warwickshire's great walkers, his long ex-guardsman's legs making easy going of lanes and fieldpaths throughout the county.

From Walcot a fordrough, a fieldpath, and a narrow stretch of dense woodland through Withycombe Wood, a riot of bluebells in season, will test your map-reading on the mile or so to Billesley, where the Tudor manor house is enclosed by a tall wall. There are those who say that Shakespeare wrote *As You Like It* here in the library, but the house as we see it was largely built in the seventeenth century by Sir Robert Lee. Hard by, All Saints Church, shaded by limes and chestnuts, was built in 1692 on the site of an earlier one where Shakespeare's granddaughter, Elizabeth Nash, married John Barnard.

From Billesley, with 14 miles behind him, the strenuous walker might choose another five miles footslog back to his starting point. Otherwise, Billesley is only half a mile from a bus or hitching route into Stratford.

Alcester is the obvious centre for the westernmost tract of Warwickshire lying along the old Ryknild Street where the land rises steadily from the River Arrow to the Ridgeway, which carries both the Redditch-Evesham road and the county boundary with Worcestershire for six upland miles. The town itself flourished as Alauna in Roman times, though its character today comes from the seventeenth and eighteenth centuries, in dormers, bow windows, and the fine Georgian group opposite the east end of the church which includes Angel House, once a coaching inn of that name with an obvious arched entrance to the stable yard. For contrast, Malt Mill Lane is as authentic Tudor as we have in the county, a street with nothing mock or restored in its atmosphere. Next door to the 'Turk's Head' on the High Street-Church Street corner the date 1525 appears among Tudor barge-boarding. Meeting Street, Butter Street and Bleachfield Street all evoke something from Alcester's past. The signs of the 'Bear', the 'Royal Oak', and the 'Cross Keys' all add colour to the present.

The Town Hall, isolated beyond the north wall of the churchyard, bears a plaque telling us that the hall, rebuilt in 1641, was purchased by public subscription from the Lord of the Manor as a memorial to the men of Alcester and Oversley who died in the First World War. The inscription is signed by the High Bailiff and the Low Bailiff of Alcester, officials of the Court Leet, a thirteenth-century survival which, though having no executive powers, still elects its officers annually including an ale-taster and a bread-weigher.

Alcester Church is one of Warwickshire's many dedications to

St. Nicholas, a great favourite as a patronal saint. Normally shown with three money bags or three golden balls, he appears in an Alcester window with three apples—a corruption of the more customary attributes.

At Arrow, half a mile along the Evesham road from Alcester are the gates of Ragley Hall, the stately home of the eighth Marquis of Hertford.

'The more recent of my ancestors are buried in Arrow Church', he once told me, 'the more ancient in the Tower, without their heads.'

The family name of the marquis is Seymour, pronounced Seamer —Hertford is rendered as Harford—and the Seymours were great intriguers in Tudor times. A Sir John Seymour married a descendant of Lionel, Duke of Clarence, son of Edward III. Their daughter, Lady Jane Seymour, third wife of Henry VIII died still a queen, but her two brothers enacted a shocking tragedy. The one, Edward, Earl of Hertford and Duke of Somerset, was Protector during the minority of his nephew, Edward VI. The other, Lord Thomas Seymour of Sudeley Castle, near Winchcombe, Gloucestershire, was the second husband of Catherine Parr, the sixth wife, who survived Henry VIII. An ambitious man, Thomas set his sights higher than a dowager queen—on no less a personage than the Princess Elizabeth. When his wife died Thomas was suspected of having poisoned her, charged with treason, and sentenced to death by his brother Somerset, who in turn was beheaded in 1552 on the warrant of John Dudley, Duke of Northumberland, his son-in-law's father.

Although Queen Elizabeth restored the earldom of Hertford to Somerset's son by a second marriage, she sent him and his wife, Lady Katherine Grey, to the Tower on their marriage, though the earl was set free on the payment of £15,000 after his wife's death. Their grandson, William, served Charles I faithfully during the Great Civil War, and was created Duke of Somerset and Marquis of Hertford, though the dukedom ceased with an unmarried seventh duke.

Meanwhile six successive Sir Edward Seymours, descended from Protector Somerset's son by his first marriage, had culminated in the reign of William III in a Speaker of the House of Commons. His second wife inherited Ragley Hall, begun about 1680 by Robert Hooke for her relative the Earl of Conway. Lady Seymour passed it to her son Francis, who was created Baron Conway. With Ragley in the family, the second Baron Conway was created Marquis of Hertford. Married to Lady Isabella Fitzroy, great granddaughter of Charles II, he found time both to run a mistress, Barbara Villiers, and to develop Ragley Hall much as we know it today.

The 3rd Marquis married an Italian heiress, Maria Fagniani, about whose paternity there was some confusion, for two millionaires claimed she was their daughter and left her their fortunes. Her son, Richard, the 4th Marquis of Hertford, inherited this fabulous wealth, but, never marrying, bequeathed it all in 1870 to his illegitimate son, Richard Wallace. The title, with Ragley Hall, Conway Castle, and some property in Coventry, went to his cousin, General Francis Seymour. This divorce between the money and the hall has confronted subsequent marquises with tremendous problems of upkeep, which would have been worse for the present holder of the title had his father not predeceased his elder brother, the 7th Marquis, by only eight months, thus avoiding one set of death duties.

The Seymour fortune that went to Richard Wallace eventually found its way to the nation in the form of the famous Wallace Collection of pictures, and the art lover in the 8th Marquis says with a forgiving smile, 'Wallace spent millions of my family's money on pictures.'

It was the Prince Regent, visiting Ragley Hall, who remarked to the 2nd Marquis that the view from his front door would be improved by a castle. The royal suggestion was taken up, and the folly known as Oversley Castle now embellishes the wooded ridge across the River Arrow.

With the Ragley parkland on the right, its beeches and oaks showering gold on the road each autumn, we carry on for four miles to Iron Cross, where the Queen's Head, with a playing-card sign, stands on the corner of a lane leading to Bevington Waste, a little-known salient of Warwickshire, a bowl of unhedged smallholdings, with wide views into Worcestershire of regiments of fruit trees marching tidily up gentle slopes. Here is a splendid miniature walking country off the beaten track. Just to northward, Weethley Wood has often given me the butterfly orchid, while the rare crimson vetchling proliferates thereabouts with the dyers greenweed like tiny bushes of broom.

Across the Alcester road is the village of Salford Priors where the church is a gem, its strongest suit being heraldry. A well-kept memorial to the Clarkes in the sanctuary glows with shields full of heraldic devices to seduce the enthusiast from whatever else he intended doing, and to make the uninitiated regret his ignorance of the subject. Here too, more readily comprehensible, a seventeenth-century grandmother and grandchild face each other across the chancel. When three-year-old Margaret, granddaughter of Sir Simon Clarke, died in 1640, her grandmother, Lady Dorothy, raised the memorial which bears the verse:

> As careful nurses to their bed do lay
> Their children which too long would wantons play;
> So to prevent all my insuing crimes,
> Nature, my nurse, laid me to bed betimes.

When her time came Lady Dorothy was commemorated across the chancel—a recumbent figure in a simple but striking red gown.

The Arrow joins the Avon at Salford Priors, which gets its name as the place where the Salt Way forded the Avon. Above the south wall of the church is a smaller tower where once a beacon glowed to direct travellers across the ford. In the churchyard a modern headstone gives an object lesson in heraldry. It commemorates Helen Mary Evershed who died in 1953. Her arms are portrayed in the diamond-shaped lozenge used by women in place of the male shield, and the knot of ribbon proclaims Helen to have been unmarried.

South-westward of the church is a field known as the Vineyard because the monks of Salford Hall once grew grapes there. Completed in its present beauty in 1606, it incorporates part of a fifteenth-century house which belonged to the abbots of Evesham, giving the name Abbots Salford to the village. Because it was occupied in 1808-30 by a sisterhood of nuns from Cambrai the hall was long known as the Nunnery. In 1970 it had become an attractive restaurant.

Coughton Court, just north of Alcester, is one of Warwickshire's famous stately homes—the seat of the Throckmortons. It is a splendid sight seen down the elm avenue planted in 1893 on the 21st birthday of Nicholas William, the 9th Baronet, but as I write the trees are threatened with the Dutch elm disease which has devastated Worcestershire.

The best-known episode in Coughton's history occurred in 1605 when the wives of several of the Gunpowder plotters were assembled there. The Gunpowder Plot was a Catholic plot, and so was the Throckmorton Plot in 1583 which sent Francis Throckmorton to the rack and execution in the Tower. But Sir Nicholas Throckmorton, who was tried for complicity in Wyatt's rebellion against Mary Tudor, was a staunch Protestant, and in 1598, Job Throckmorton, a deep-dyed Puritan, was arrested under suspicion of being 'Martin Marprelate', author of ribald tracts against priests and bishops. Author or no, he certainly set up the secret printing press on which the tracts were produced in his manor at Haseley, near Warwick. Job's father, Clement Throckmorton of Kenilworth, built the old Haseley Manor in 1561 on ground bought from his uncle, Michael Throckmorton, who received it from Mary Tudor for his services in Italy, where he was sent to spy on Cardinal Pole but remained as his loyal secretary.

Clement Throckmorton was cup-bearer to Katherine Parr. He lies buried with his wife, Katherine Nevill, in Haseley Church beneath a slate slab with fine brasses which depict Clement in full Elizabethan armour with sword and dagger, and Katherine in detailed costume. At their feet are smaller brasses of their six sons and seven daughters, that of the sons being a palimpsest, hinged so that it can be lifted to reveal earlier engravings on the reverse. Clement died in 1573, Job in 1601, and several generations later Haseley went out of the Throckmorton family though the initials C.T. and K.N. still appear on the porch spandrels and, until it was removed to Coughton some years ago, the Throckmorton arms decorated the fireplace, crowned by a falcon crest. It may not be entirely coincidence that the nearest inn at Haseley is the 'Falcon', where Tom Dollery, former Warwickshire cricket captain is host.

So back to Coughton Court and the main Throckmorton line, whose crest is an elephant's head. Clement was one of eight sons of Sir George Throckmorton, himself being the great grandson of John Throckmorton, who, by marrying an heiress of the Spiney family in 1409, brought her estate at Coughton into his family. Previously the Throckmortons lived at Throckmorton in Fladbury parish, Worcestershire, and at Fladbury Church John is buried with his ancestors. He was Under Treasurer of England, died in 1445, and Throgmorton Street, the London home of the Stock Exchange, is named after him. The most famous of Sir George's sons was the above-mentioned Sir Nicholas. Lucky to escape with his life after the Wyatt rebellion, he became Elizabeth's ambassador to France and Spain, though his relations with that fiery queen were prickly at times.

'God's death, villain, I will have thy head', she once stormed at him. Unruffled, Sir Nicholas replied: 'You will do well, Madam, to consider in that case how you will afterwards keep your own on your shoulders'.

The most widely known Throckmorton today—though those who know of her may not all appreciate that she was an historical figure —is a daughter of Sir Nicholas, Bessie Throckmorton, the English rose of *Merrie England*. Bessie was a maid of honour to Elizabeth, and her clandestine marriage to Sir Walter Raleigh in 1592 caused the outraged queen to send them both to the Tower. Bessie has been described as 'charming in person, tall, slender, golden-haired and blue-eyed, and inheriting all the courage of her father'.

Standing alongside Coughton Court is the church built by Sir Robert Throckmorton, father of Sir George. In the nave Sir Robert installed his own tomb, but he died in 1518 in the Holy Land, and the tomb remained empty until 1791 when Sir Robert, the 4th Baronet, was buried in it, as is also his successor, Sir John. The great Sir George, who built the lovely gatehouse at Coughton in the reign of Henry VIII, also lies in the church with his wife, Catherine Vaux, their epitaph explaining that they lived to 1553, long enough to see 112 grandchildren from their eight sons and 11 daughters.

The Throckmorton baronetcy was conferred on Sir Robert in 1642 by Charles I and, subsequently Coughton Court suffered for its loyalty to the king. Parliament forces occupied it in October 1643, and when Royalists bombarded them four months later it was badly damaged. Repairs were scarcely complete when the house was ravaged again by a 'Protestant mob' from Alcester on Running Thursday, when James II fled the throne in 1688. It was a century before the damage was cleared, but meantime Sir Robert, the 3rd Baronet, had married Mary Yate, through whom Buckland in Berkshire and Harvington Hall, the famous Worcestershire house, accrued to the Throckmortons. Harvington was sold in 1923, but in 1910 a magnificent staircase had been brought from there for the newly-established saloon at Coughton.

With its memories of Father Wall and other priests who hid in Harvington's honeycomb of secret rooms, the staircase is one of Coughton's array of Catholic mementoes along with the chemise worn by Mary, Queen of Scots, at her execution. But Coughton's most famous article of clothing is the Throckmorton Coat, converted from the covering on sheep's backs to that of the 5th Baronet, Sir John, between sunrise and sunset on 25 June 1811, and all done by hand. At five a.m. Sir John's shepherd sheared two sheep, and at Greenham Mills, near Newbury, their wool was spun, and the yarn spooled, warped, loomed and woven. The cloth was then processed by four p.m. Within a further two hours and 20 minutes James White, a tailor, cut out and made up the coat, in which Sir John appeared before 5,000 spectators 13 hours and 20 minutes after it was wool on the sheep's backs.

Sir John, Sir George, and Sir Charles, 5th, 6th and 7th Baronets, were brothers. Sir Charles died in 1850, and when his tomb was being constructed in Coughton Church the remains were discovered of Dame Elizabeth Throckmorton and two nuns. She was the last Abbess of Denny, Cambridgeshire, and when her abbey was 'dissolved' in 1539 she came with her companions to Coughton where, as near as possible, they followed the rule of their order for eight years. Their bones now lie with those of Sir Charles in the church built by the abbess's brother, Sir Robert. History repeated itself at Coughton after 350 years when, in 1860, another Sir Robert, the 8th Baronet, built the Catholic church which completes the trio of buildings there.

The present holder of the title is also a Sir Robert. His father was killed in action in Mesopotamia on 9 April 1916, on which day, by tragic coincidence, a stone shield bearing the family arms fell from the gatehouse at Coughton and was broken. Many more Throckmortons hang among the 77 family portraits which can be seen at Coughton Court by permission of Sir Robert, for though the house was handed to the National Trust in 1945 the contents belong to the family.

And, the pronunciation is Co-ton.

71

CHAPTER FOUR

Edgehill and Compton Wynyates

It is more than an arbitrary county boundary that marks the traveller's passage from Warwickshire into Oxfordshire as he speeds south towards Banbury. Sunrising Hill or Warmington Hill mark a transition from the lowland Lower Lias clays of the Feldon to a new upland world (in Oxfordshire) of Middle Lias Marlstone, only a small salient of which thrusts into Warwickshire on the wooded Edgehill escarpment. Two Warwickshire villages are trapped up in this brown ironstone country.

Shotteswell, one of them, is called locally 'Satchel', and most people know it as merely the pointed end of a pepper-pot steeple peeping from below ground level at the far side of a field on the left of the Warwick-Banbury road two miles past Warmington Hill. The church, set haphazardly on a steep slope with the other village buildings, all the colour of old mustard, illustrates vividly the origin of the saying 'The weakest go to the wall'. It was not customary to sit during services in bygone days, the congregation standing or kneeling. Round the walls of some churches were stone benches, and at the commencement of his sermon the preacher would say 'Let the weakest go to the wall', whereupon the aged and the infirm would be seated on the wall benches such as Shotteswell has in the north aisle. Among the lords of the manor of Shotteswell were the North family. One clergyman to whom they presented the living was a bit of a wag, and he took as the text of his first sermon the seventh verse of Psalm 75 : 'Promotion cometh neither from the east, nor from the west, nor yet from the south.'

Ratley, the other Warwickshire village up among the ironstone, might well have inspired the wartime song 'There'll always be an England'. Thirteen fighting Englands survived the First World War, and four died that England might live. Their 17 names are recorded on the war memorial in Ratley Church, and still the Englands proliferate in the village.

It was in Ratley that I found a gem of village social history, a small notebook entitled 'The Visiting List of the Rev. A. Child', which contains, neatly written, a register of every soul in each house in the parish in walking order with instructions for the itinerary. Every parishioner's age is given as in 1881, with a 'b' or 'c' for baptized or confirmed. Mr. Child makes the occasional comment— as of Drusilla Prue: 'Has buried three husbands; gifted with the needle'. Beside the name of Ezekial Horseley, a stonepit workman, is the one damning word 'Drinks'. The book has 18 separate England entries. George England's family, then living at Churchyard Cottage, numbered 12 children, and of his wife Mary it was written: 'nee Batchelor, dressmaker, goitre.' Several goitres are recorded among women, maybe due to the spring water running through the local ironstone. One prolific spring, the Goggles, still spouts from a bank beside the churchyard. It is impossible to sort out the Englands of 1881 into relationships. There was a 'Long David' England and a 'Short David' England who had a donkey and cart with which he travelled round shaping wall stone. He had a son, Eleazer—'A good sort of rough fellow' according to the old vicar's book. A Joseph and Anna England kept the 'Rose and Crown' at Ratley—still going strong—and one of their sons, Eli, was landlord of the pub in nearby Warmington.

Only one England died in World War Two, his name being duly added on the churchyard cross. One addition has been made since, of a villager killed in Cyprus in 1957—a Private French.

Some Ratley men are among the 30 or so employed at Hornton Quarries on Edgehill, where the stone is not only quarried, but worked to a high standard for building, memorial, and garden purposes by craftsmen masons.

Among the Edgehill beeches rises an octagonal battlemented tower. Built in 1749 by Sanderson Miller of Radway Grange at the foot of Edgehill, it is incorporated in the Castle Inn, where hang pistols, swords, and breastplates dug up from the battlefield below. But if anyone tells you that Charles 1 watched the Battle of Edgehill from the tower, remind him that it was built 107 years after the battle, which took place on Sunday, 23 October 1642.

73

Four days earlier 11,000 infantry, 2,000 cavalry, and 1,000 dragoons set out from Worcester under Robert Devereux, 3rd Earl of Essex, Commander-in-Chief of the Parliamentary forces. His personal belongings included his coffin, his winding sheet, and his funeral hatchment—morbid tokens of his determination to serve his masters at Westminster faithfully unto death. His immediate intention was to interpose his army between Charles I with the Royalist forces who were marching from Shrewsbury, and London, where supporters of the King were openly wearing red Cavalier favours in their hats in expectation of his coming. Charles left Shrewsbury on 12 October and, marching via Bridgnorth and Wolverhampton, had slept at Aston Hall, Birmingham, on Monday night, 17 October. On the night of the 19th he was at Kenilworth, and by the 22nd at Edgcote, near Chipping Warden. Here he was joined by his dashing nephew, Prince Rupert, who, moving in from Stourbridge, had fought a skirmish with some Parliamentarians around King's Norton, on the outskirts of Birmingham.

Essex was at Kineton, beneath Edgehill, on the night of the 22nd. So Charles was ahead in the race for London, but not wishing to appear to be running from the enemy, he moved seven miles westward and deployed his army for battle on the steep escarpment at Edgehill, as the bells rang for Sunday morning church. The ridge had fewer trees in 1642, and the 14,000 Royalists had a good view of their 10,000 foes in the plain below. Today almost the entire battlefield is enclosed in a vast army camp. Charles stationed himself early on at Knowle End, where the Kineton-Banbury road curves up the north-eastern flank of Edgehill. There the guns were trained on him, and the spot is now known as Bullet Hill, being marked until recently by a ragged copse of hawthorn in the shape of a crown.

The dour Parliamentarians must have proved an unexpectedly colourful sight as the King surveyed them. Four of their regiments were identified by favours of red, purple, blue, and grey, while Hampden's troops, not yet on the field, were distinguished by green. All wore orange armbands, and dark-clad preachers moved among their ranks. With the Royalists was old Sir Jacob Astley whose prayer before the battle was 'Lord, thou knowest how busy I must be this day. If I forget Thee, do not Thou forget me.'

Soon after midday the Royalists advanced downhill and operations

14 *Tudor England still endures at Compton Wynyates, home of the Marquess of Northampton*

commenced—badly for Essex, from whose army one entire troop deserted to the King, led ironically by one Sir Faithful Fortescue. Rupert on the Royalist right and Wilmot on the left charged with their cavalry, while the infantry in the centre came to 'push of pike', locked in a close struggle. Rupert routed his opponents, chasing them two miles beyond Kineton before returning to the battlefield. Wilmot shattered Parliament's extreme right but by-passed two enemy cavalry regiments which, remaining the only horsemen on the field, badly mauled the King's infantry. At one point the royal standard was captured and its bearer, Sir Edmund Verney, slain. It was recovered later in fighting around a mound of five trees now growing beside the road from Radway to Westcote Farm.

Hostilities broke off at dusk, and Charles spent the night in King's Leys Barn, his cold and hungry forces around him. Essex and his men found more comfortable billets in Kineton. Charles was prepared to renew the fight on 24 October, but Essex withdrew to Warwick, having failed to stop the King's march to London. This was resumed without further opposition, though it stopped short with the King's triumphal entrance into Oxford.

News of the battle had reached London quickly. A fire, blazing on the beacon which still crowns the Burton Dassett Hills just eastward of Edgehill, kindled a fiery chain which sped news of a Royalist victory southward. Though the King had lost more of the total slain—put at any figure between 1,000 and 5,000—the enemy had not stopped his march. One victim, Henry Kingsmill, a Royalist Captain of Foot, has a memorial in Radway Church where his epitaph ends : 'I have fought a good fight. I have finished my course. Hereafter is laid up for me a crown of righteousness.' Hundreds more lie buried in Graveground Coppice in the army camp. In 1949 two identical pillars were erected by Warwickshire County Council to commemorate the battle. They stand three quarters of a mile apart, one in the camp, the other on the grass verge of the B4451.

Barely 100 yards from the pillar in the camp is Warwickshire's least-known memorial, hidden as it is from the public. It commemorates the death on 9 April 1892 of Captain W. G. 'Bay' Middleton of Hazelbeach, Northants, who was thrown from his horse, Night Line, during the Midland Sportsmen's point-to-point. A durable marble slab marks the spot where Captain Middleton fell.

15 *The spacious Feldon from Edgehill above Arlescote Manor*

Chains surround it and the wind sighs through four pines above. With Graveground Coppice hard by it is an eerie spot, and there I spent the night of the 310th anniversary of the Battle of Edgehill on 23 October 1952. Legend has it that on each anniversary the ghosts of the slain rise from their communal grave and fight it out again. I was unlucky. They slept soundly when I kept vigil there.

Radway, a picturesque village, has an association with bloodier battles than Edgehill. The lych gate at the church with a graceful broach spire, is a memorial to the villagers who fought in the First World War, and among the 44 who returned, listed alphabetically, is the name of 'Haig—Field Marshal Earl', who went from his home at Radway Grange to become Commander-in-Chief in Flanders.

The sons of Charles I, later Charles II and James II, were at Edgehill as boys under the care of their tutor, Dr. William Harvey, who discovered the circulation of the blood. They were lodged in Arlescote Manor, situated cosily under the north-eastern shoulder of Edgehill, and the name 'Charles', scratched on a window pane in a cursive Jacobean hand, was thought to be the work of the young prince. The glass was removed and taken from Arlescote to Bristol by a one-time occupant of the manor, where an earlier royal cipher still appears in some old window fasteners which open to the shape of 'E.R.'—Edward VI Rex. As seen today, with gazebos in the angle of the garden walls, Arlescote Manor is the result of seventeenth-century alterations in which Inigo Jones had some part.

South-westward of Radway the foot of the Edgehill escarpment is called the Vale of Red Horse because of a mysterious hill figure once cut on the russet slopes near Sunrising Hill. An unlikely legend has it that it was cut by Warwick, the Kingmaker, in memory of his charger which he slew rather than retreat at the Battle of Towton. Once yearly, on Palm Sunday, the figure was cleaned up, and after the original was destroyed in 1798 at the Enclosure of open fields, the landlord of the 'Sunrising Inn' is reputed to have cut another because his pub did such good trade on the day of the annual clean-up.

Upton House, just back from the escarpment hereabouts, was given to the National Trust by Lord Bearsted in 1948, and is famous for its 200 pictures and its gardens. In the mid-eighteenth century Robert Child, a wealthy banker, purchased the estate. When the Earl of Westmorland and Child's daughter, Sarah Anne, fell in love the banker withheld his consent to a marriage. Some time later the earl casually asked Child a seemingly hypothetical question as to what he, the banker, would do if he loved a girl and the father opposed the match. Child replied that he would elope with the girl; advice which was taken a few days later when the banker found himself chasing his daughter and the earl to Gretna Green. Too late to prevent the marriage, he swore his wealth would never go to the impoverished Westmorland title, and eventually he left his money and Upton to his daughter's second surviving child, Sarah, who became the wife of George, 5th Earl of Jersey.

The Vale of Red Horse is a countryside of large fields given a further spaciousness by unfenced roads. Oxhill and Middle Tysoe both have a Peacock Inn with splendid signs, one side of each showing the bird trailing its tail, while the reverse shows the peacock in his pride, the tail spread in all its glory. Oxhill has much that is Norman in its church, but, as so often, it is epitaphs that provide the greatest interest. Daniel Beckford, a Royalist officer, died in 1681, and his verse reads:

> *When I was young I ventured life and blood*
> *Both for my King and for my Country's good:*
> *In older years my care was chief to be*
> *Soldier to Him that shed his blood for me.*

Off the south-east corner of Oxhill Church is the 'Slave's Grave'. Here rests a negro boy, servant at nearby Whitehill Farm, his tiny headstone inscribed: 'Here lieth the body of Nartilla, negro slave to Mr. Beauchamp of Nevis, Baptised October 20, Buried January 26, 1796.'

Pillerton Hersey, three miles northward, has a lengthy epitaph to a village worthy who died in 1852. It begins:

> *Here lies old William Allibone,*
> *Our venerable wheelwright gone;*
> *Oft as each Christian neighbour fell,*
> *Studious he shaped each homely shell*
> *To order of the passing bell,*
> *And each poor soul he gently gave*
> *On slackened cordage to the grave....*

An unlucky chance in this wide and unpopulous landscape led a German bomb in 1941 to destroy part of Whatcote Church, including a Norman font. But there are other Norman fonts, and mercifully the probably unique item at Whatcote survived, a mural memorial to the Rev. John Davenport, incumbent there for 70½ years—which could well be a record—until his death, aged 101 in 1668. The churchyard at Winderton hereabouts provides a plum for collectors of graveyard curiosities in the smart new headstone inscribed MISTER MAYCOCK. Rather bald, I thought, until enquiries revealed MISTER to be his Christian name. He was, in fact, Mr. Mister Maycock. More remarkable, his wife was, I suppose, Mrs. Mister Maycock.

St. Mary's Church at Middle Tysoe redeems the colourless and dreary churches without stained glass around Edgehill. It abounds in interest, with brasses, bosses, corbels, the remains of a rood loft, and, among many saints in the windows, an outstanding St. Christopher, a memorial to the Rev. Christopher Dunkin Francis, vicar from 1852-95.

At the south-western extremity of its five-mile ridge Edgehill breaks up into a strange and memorable landscape of small symmetrical grassy hills: Shenlow Hill, Epwell Hill, Yarn Hill and others Excepting Tysoe Hill these are just across the Oxfordshire border, but they are so much part of the view from the Warwickshire plain beneath them as to merit mention.

The quality of some buildings depends on your coming upon them initially from just the right place. This applies so much to Warwickshire's most lovely stately home, Compton Wynyates, that, should you approach it in orthodox fashion by the road west of it, do continue past the entrance, uphill, until between the trees you see the many-chimneyed battlemented sixteenth-century house fronted by its shaped yews below you. Better still, come to it by your own effort, afoot, up the fields from Upper Tysoe. The route is obvious through the gate just beyond the village, strikes up to the Marquis of Northampton's restored windmill, its sails set in the form of a St. Andrew's Cross as windmill sails were always set on Sundays and holidays. As you reach the sheltering hedge of hawthorn surrounding it the view opens up on the other side of the hill, and there, embowered in trees, lies Compton Wynyates, described in Sir Nikolaus

Pevsner's *Warwickshire* as 'the perfect picture-book house of the Early Tudor decades, the most perfect in England in the specific picturesque completely irregular mode.'

But whichever way you approach Compton Wynyates breathe a prayer of gratitude to John Berrill. In the church hard by the house there is a small bronze plaque to his memory in the floor. He deserves something greater. Steward to the Earl of Northampton at Compton Wynyates for 32 years, Berrill saved the house when it might have been demolished. In 1768 the 8th Earl spent so much on election expenses as parliamentary candidate for Northampton that he had to sell his furniture and fell his timber to repay the debts he incurred. After years of financial difficulty he went to live quietly in Switzerland, leaving orders that Compton Wynyates be pulled down. Berrill turned a deaf ear. Though the house remained empty he kept out the weather and bricked up the windows to avoid the window tax, confident that the family would return to 'Compton-in-the-Hole' some day. Return they did, promoted to a marquisate, the extravagant earl's son, Charles, being created Marquis of Northampton by George III in 1812.

Berrill's memorial tells a sad story. John died, aged 64, on 15 October 1834, his wife, Hannah, aged 41, only 16 days later, and their daughter Augusta, aged only 18 months, on 2 December 1834.

The recipient of the first earldom of Northampton in 1618 was William, the second Lord Compton. His son, who succeeded to the earldom in 1630, was named Spencer, and how he came by that forename involves an amusing love story culminating in the 'baker's basket elopement'. William's father, Sir Henry Compton, was a favourite of Queen Elizabeth, whom he entertained at Compton Wynyates in 1572, for which she created him Baron Compton. William himself continued to serve at Court after inheriting the title in 1589. Even so, despite Compton Wynyates and Castle Ashby, with other property in 20 counties; despite his nearness to the Queen; the spirited young courtier was regarded as a poor match for his only child, Elizabeth, by Sir John Spencer, Lord Mayor of London in 1593, and one of the wealthiest men in Britain.

The girl returned William's love and so, for a time, she was sent into hiding. But William was a determined man. Spying carefully at Elizabeth's London home, he realised that the baker paid a regular visit with a particularly large bread basket. A generous bribe, and the baker was his man. Disguising himself, and wearing the baker's apron, Lord Compton hauled the bread basket into the Spencer home. Emptying out the loaves, he met Elizabeth, tucked her in his basket, covered her up, and was staggering downstairs with his burden when, to his horror, he met Sir John. But the disguise was good. Not only did Sir John fail to penetrate it, he even gave the noble 'baker' a sixpence, congratulated him on being so early, and assured him that such diligence would bring him success in life. Not unnaturally, when Sir John learned how he had been tricked he was extremely angry and disinherited his daughter. Then, in May 1601, the imperious Queen Elizabeth commanded him to adopt a child for whom she would stand sponsor. Tricked yet again, Sir John found himself adopting his own grandson, Spencer Compton, offspring of William and his daughter Elizabeth. He accepted the inevitable, was reconciled with his daughter, and when he died in 1610, left his son-in-law £300,000—with astonishing results.

A contemporary writer reported that Lord Compton 'oppressed with the greatness of his sudden fortunes' fell mad. The Earl of Suffolk tried to seize his money, but Compton soon recovered, set about getting through his windfall, and 'did within less than eight weeks spend £72,000, most in great horses, rich saddles, and play'. In 1618 he was created Earl of Northampton by James I, and when, ten years later, he was elected a Knight of the Garter, he rode from London to Windsor with so splendid an equipage that he was accorded a vote of thanks by the Order.

The son of so lively a wooing as the 'bread basket elopement' himself proved a spirited character. Spencer became M.P. for Ludlow and Master of the Robes to Charles I both as prince and king. He succeeded to the earldom in 1630. When the Great Civil War broke out he went, in 1642, with the king to York and was impeached by Parliament for his refusal to return to London. After an attempt to surprise the Roundhead stronghold at Warwick Castle he took Banbury Castle, where his third son, another William, was given command. This William is buried at Compton Wynyates, a memorial in the church setting forth his military attainments.

Spencer also raised a regiment of horse commanded by his eldest son, James, in which his second son, Charles, served. Charles inherited his grandfather's aptitude for disguise, though in war rather than in love, for, heavily disguised, he and six followers penetrated Beeston Castle in Cheshire, cut down the drawbridge, seized the outworks, and captured 30 Roundhead soldiers—but had to withdraw for lack of support. Spencer fought at Edgehill, but in 1643 he was killed leading a Royalist charge with his customary dash at Hopton Heath, near Stafford. His cavalry routed their opposite numbers, but the enemy foot stood firm. The earl's charger fell beneath him and, refusing quarter, he was knocked out with a musket, his body stripped, and taken to Uttoxeter. His son, James, recovered the body in exchange for all the ammunition, cannon, and prisoners taken by the King's forces at Hopton Heath.

Compton Wynyates, home of these doughty fighters, became the object of a Roundhead attack, falling in 1644 to Colonel Purefoy after a fight lasting two days during which the Parliamentarians killed all the deer in the park and damaged memorials in the church. The Countess of Northampton tended a number of wounded Royalists hiding in the roof of Compton Wynyates, and helped them escape when they recovered. In addition to the three sons already mentioned, Spencer had three younger sons. The fourth and fifth were also Royalist soldiers, but, by a crowning irony, Henry, youngest son of this family so devoted to the Stuart kings, became Bishop of London and, in 1688, crowned William and Mary, after the abdication of James II.

We must retrace our steps along Edgehill to take in a felicitous tract of country east of the Banbury road, with Warmington Church atop its hill where labouring lorries, bound for Oxford, gasp out their last breaths of diesel fumes. Despite this constant industrial stream the church has an eerie atmosphere, emanating, one wonders, from Captain Gaudin and 12 troopers slain betimes at Edgehill and buried in the churchyard. Not that I have ever found their headstones; this scabrous yellow-brown ironstone is surely the worst memorial stone in Britain, erupting in a greyish mould which renders inscriptions almost illegible. Adding to a pervasive unhappiness in the church is the saga of tragedy which befell the Rev. William Harrison in his 46 years as vicar. Four of his children died young, while a fifth, an ensign of the 11th Regiment, was 'accidentally drowned in his passage to Australia'.

Warmington village lies in a hollow beneath the church, one of the most snug and attractive villages in the county, built round a spacious triangular green with the manor house dominating the south side above a pond. Built around 1600 it has symmetrical gabled wings with windows to three storeys. Almost central between them, a strange feature so prominent in the façade of a house, is a wide chimney-breast. Long before this manor house was built, there were 20 tenants of the monkish lords of the manor who had built their own cell on the hillside. Each tenant sent a labourer every week-day to work for the monks, or paid one penny fine. Each harnessed a team to plough the monks' land on three days annually, and, among other duties, each tenant provided cartage once a year for a wagon-load of the monks' hay or corn to Warwick.

When England was engaged in the Hundred Years War the French monasteries lost their lands in England lest they become a fifth column, so the monks of Warmington, who belonged to a foundation at Preux in Normandy, were expelled, and the lordship of the manor of Warmington was bestowed instead on the monks of Wytham in Somerset.

Two miles north-east of Warmington the grounds of Farnborough Hall overflow across the public road in well-cut lawns and a lake. In 1684 the hall became the home of the Holbech family, who were also lords of the manor of Mollington, the neighbouring village across the Oxfordshire border. When the two properties were left respectively to the brothers William and Hugh, so great was their affection that William laid out the terrace walk and, at an appointed hour each morning, walked to the far end for a chat with his brother where their estates met. The Farnborough obelisk was built at the same time—in 1751—though it has since been rebuilt. The hall is now a National Trust property.

In Farnborough Church there are memorials to a Holbech who was Bishop of St. Helena, and to Holbech soldiers, but, beneath a hedge where a path leads out from the north-east corner of the churchyard, it is a humble cross that has a poignancy lacking in the grander monuments. Inscribed simply 'I was a stranger and ye took me in', it marks the grave of an unidentified tramp who wandered into the village and died. Farnborough is a pleasant village with its thatch and yellow stone; above all else a sylvan place.

84

Ineradicably etched on my memory is the tracery of Edgehill's bare trees against the afterglow of a bitter but beautiful winter's day as I walked from Farnborough the mile and a half of road to Avon Dassett, and so on to the lilliputian Burton Dassett Hills. Just as Edgehill dissolves at its south-west end in the hillocks of Oxfordshire, so its north-eastern extremity is marked by more little hills, though these, the Burton Dassetts, form a much better-integrated miniature range, with their own church and beacon tower to add character to them, while kindly nature is steadily covering the evidence that they were once extensively quarried for ironstone. The beacon had as neighbour a windmill until it was blown down in 1946, fortunately without the tragedy that attended the destruction of its predecessor in a storm in 1655, when the miller was killed while trying to turn the sails into the wind. The carpenter, Will Whitehead, and the mason, John Basse, who built the later windmill, lie in Burton Dassett churchyard, their headstones decorated with the tools of their trades.

Burton Dassett Church is unusual in that it climbs steadily uphill by six separate sets of steps from the west end to the altar. Roomy, bare, and without coloured glass, it has two Norman doorways and a whole menagerie of animals carved around the capitals in the north arcade, rabbits, a squirrel, dragons, some upside down. Its ecclesiastical history is equally fascinating. In 1646, while the vicar, Robert Kenwrick, was away serving in the Royalist forces, Parliament sent in its own minister, Nathaniel Partridge, and with him the *Burton Directory of Publique Worship* to replace the Book of Common Prayer. The use of the *Directory* was discontinued in 1662, but it is still displayed in the church, the only copy known to be preserved in the parish to which it was originally sent. For some years it lay beneath the bed of the village blacksmith and parish clerk, Thomas Basse, who refused to surrender it when Partridge's successor, the much-loved Thomas Mansell, was replaced after the Restoration by a Royalist vicar, Chamberlain Hammersley. Not until he was on his deathbed did Basse send for Hammersley to restore the *Directory* and the parish registers to him.

The parish of Burton Dassett included hamlets at either end of the hills—Northend with Knightcote, and Southend with Little Dassett—the church standing at Southend. In the fifteenth century when, despite the Wars of the Roses, Burton Dassett was a prosperous market town, an orphan boy, John Kimble, came begging one day, but was spurned by the people of Southend though at Northend he was most hospitably received. Kimble became a farmer at Mollington and prospered. By his will in 1469 he left a dole to the kindly villagers of Northend, and down the centuries Northend and Knightcote have benefited from the John Kimble Charity, by a school with a stipend for the schoolmaster, a supply of spring water from the hills, coal and food for the sick and needy, and by a distribution of bread on New Year's Day, still continued with help to any villager entering hospital, and national saving certificates given annually to the children.

The Burton Dassett beacon was erected by Sir Edward Belknap, an absentee lord of the manor, who evicted 12 tenant farmers and their dependants to enclose 600 acres for sheep. Southend failed to survive this depopulation, and today the church stands, practically isolated, at the far end of the hills from its Northend parishioners.

At the eastern foot of the Burton Dassetts the village of Fenny Compton has a most attractive little church with a window of interest to the railway enthusiast. It commemorates a native of the parish, Thomas Payne, who became an eminent engineer, and an inscription tells us that 'he designed and constructed the embankment across Traethmawr, as a result of which large tracts were recovered from the sea, and Portmadoc and Tremadoc originated.' This embankment is now known as The Cob, and across it the Festiniog Railway Society runs the trains which it has brought back to life as a considerable tourist attraction in North Wales.

CHAPTER FIVE

Kineton and the Verney Country

John Henry Peyto Verney, the 20th Baron Willoughby de Broke, his father, and his grandfather, have all been Master of the Warwickshire Hunt, which has its kennels at Little Kineton only three miles from the old family home of Compton Verney. In 1941 these kennels were the headquarters of the searchlight troop with which I was serving during the Midlands blitz. Once a week we took a bath at local residences kind enough to provide this facility, and he was a nonentity among his fellow artillerymen who, in this aristocratic countryside, patronized any home without a title. My bath hostess was the Hon. Mrs. Patience Hanbury, an aunt of Lord Willoughby de Broke, and, my ablutions complete, I was always given tea at her Kineton home. A pleasant village of 1,000 or so population, Kineton is the centre of a hunting country which might fairly be called the Verney Country.

The streams that spring from Edgehill and the Burton Dassett Hills come together eventually, and in Kineton assume an identity as the River Dene which pursues as charming a course as any Warwickshire river for a modest ten miles to join the Avon in Charlecote Park. Flowing eastward from Kineton it passes northward of Butlers Marston, a delightful hamlet of thatched cottages and a quiet wide street with no through way. In 1729 a villager, Miss Woodward, married a Mr. Thackeray of Hampsthwaite, Yorkshire, and their son was William Makepeace Thackeray, the novelist, who has another Warwickshire association in that the original of Becky Sharp, his heroine in *Vanity Fair*, lived at King's Coughton, near Alcester.

West of Butlers Marston, but before it reaches the Roman Fosse Way, the Dene receives the little Com Brook, coming down from Compton Verney through two lakes, the upper one spanned by the bridge of three arches which, with the surrounding cedars, sets off so graciously the old mansion of the Willoughby de Brokes above the waterside lawns. 'Capability' Brown designed the chapel at Compton Verney and might well have landscaped the grounds. An unknown architect built the west range of the house in 1714 for the 12th Lord Willoughby de Broke; Robert Adam made additions in 1760 for the 14th Baron, including the east portico of four massive Corinthian columns; and John Gibson effected certain alterations in 1855.

The first Lord Willoughby de Broke was Robert Willoughby, ennobled by Henry VII for whom he fought at Bosworth. The title came to the Verneys when Margaret Willoughby—on whom it had devolved—married Sir Richard Verney of Compton Verney in the sixteenth century. The house in which he lived was burned down, being replaced by the present building.

John, the 14th Baron, a nephew of the 13th Lord Willoughby de Broke, brought the additional surname of Peyto into the family when he succeeded in 1752. The Peytos lived at Chesterton, just off the Fosse Way, where the church has an ornate tomb of Humphrey Peyto, who died in 1585, and his wife Anne. Chesterton is better known for its unusual windmill, built as an observatory in 1632 and recently renovated, which looks down a couple of fields to eight acres surrounded by an earthwork beside the Fosse Way, probably a Roman staging camp or settlement.

Henry Verney, who became the 18th Lord Willoughby de Broke in 1862, came down from Oxford three years later to Victorian country-house life at its most spacious, his preoccupations being field sports, the captaincy of Warwickshire County Cricket Club, and the well-being of his tenantry. He numbered among his greatest friends his head gamekeeper, Jesse Eales. On the morning following their wedding, Henry and his bride were out with the Warwickshire Hounds, of which he became Master for 24 years. He commanded the 4th Troop of Warwickshire Yeomanry, and the 54 troopers were all his tenants.

The idyll broke when crops were ruined by ten wet seasons and the tenant farmers fell behind with rent, until ultimately Lord Willoughby was practically farming his entire 18,000 acres alone. He died at 58 and was succeeded by his son Richard Greville Verney, who, as successful Conservative candidate for Rugby in 1895, had driven his bride on an electioneering trip round the constituency for a honeymoon. Moving to the Lords he became one of the Diehard 'Ditchers' who fought in the last ditch against Asquith's proposal to swamp the Lords with Liberal peers unless their House passed the Parliament Bill which would curtail their own powers. In the 'Peers versus People' fight he even invited Lloyd George to visit Compton Verney and question the estate workers about their standard of living and happiness, but the offer was declined.

On Home Rule for Ireland Lord Willoughby de Broke was a staunch supporter of the Ulster Volunteers and acted as their agent in procuring arms to resist Home Rule. The more formidable conflict of the First World War brought in its train the sale of Compton Verney and 5,000 acres to Lord Manton. In the 1930s it became the property of Stanley Lamb, Junr., a cotton magnate, and since his death the estate has been further split. The present Lord Willoughby de Broke lived at Kineton and was Lord Lieutenant of Warwickshire until 1968.

A pleasant walk from Compton Verney up Spring Hill for half a mile towards Kineton before turning right along a lane unfenced on your left brings you to the remote village of Combrook. It stands on the road to nowhere, and throws several tiny bridges astride the brook, which forms the boundary between the gardens of the steep-roofed houses on either bank. Lavender borders the churchyard path, and the steeple is a weird one. A downhill road beside the church leads to a secluded row of cottages and the gate to a field where a fine vista awaits you up the lower Compton Verney lake. A public footpath west of the lake brings you back to the road—a road which, much of the way to Wellesbourne, resembles New Forest country, with wide green verges to the roadside woodlands.

West of Fosse Bridge the River Dene turns north with thick woods rising from its eastern bank as it flows through the parkland of Walton Hall. This valley is one of the exquisite gems of Warwickshire scenery, particularly when autumn has painted tints of saffron and russet on the trees of Bath Hill. A magnificent cedar sweeps the lawns immediately westward of the hall, and beyond it, across the sedge-fringed lake, ranks of sombre wellingtonias march up Spetchley Drive. Northward, beyond graceful Gog Bridge, which spans the artificially-widened river, oak- and chestnut-studded pasture stretches to the few houses of Walton village.

There was a settlement south of Walton Hall in a field called Old Town when Roman legions tramped the Fosse Way. The first evidence of a dwelling on the site of the hall is a possibly Norman cellar. A L'Estrange family lived at Walton, and into it by marriage, in the reign of Henry VIII, came one Robert Mordaunt from Bedfordshire. His grandson, L'Estrange Mordaunt, brought the red-hand badge to the Mordaunts' sable stars and chevrons in the heraldic windows of Walton Hall during the first year of the Order of Baronetcy, 1611. A line of eleven Mordaunt baronets died out with Sir Osbert L'Estrange Mordaunt in 1934, and the Walton Estate has descended to Sir Richard Hamilton, Bart, whose mother was a sister of Sir Osbert. Sir Richard and his wife, Elizabeth, live at the Old Rectory, Walton.

Throughout the eighteenth century each newly-married Mordaunt made personal alterations at Walton Hall, Sir Charles, the 6th Baronet, rebuilding the chapel in 1750, altering the house and stables, and constructing, on that wooded ridge, an octagonal room above a Roman bath, decorated as a shell grotto by Mrs. Delaney of Wellesbourne. Ultimately it was Caroline, wife of Sir John, the 9th Baronet, who during her long widowhood, employed Sir Gilbert Scott in designing the mansion standing today.

Throughout the war Walton Hall was occupied by soldiers of many nationalities and, with hostilities ceased, it remained a Territorial Army training camp specialising in Army Cadets. I was present when six of these youngsters had the shock of their lives in the summer of 1961. Some youth-club friends of mine, thinking to add a little variety to walking, had dressed up as Roman soldiers, and, 30 or so strong, spent several days marching the Fosse Way. I had gone out to meet these 'Romans', and was awaiting them where the Fosse crosses the road from Walton to Pillerton Hersey. Just as they came in sight on the Fosse, so six youngsters in uniform approached from Walton haggling over a map.

'Hi, mister', called one of them, 'is there a Roman road anywhere here?'

'Yes', I replied from the crossroads. 'I'm standing on it, and if you come up here you'll see the Romans.'

They came, with contemptuous comments of disbelief which turned to astonishment and even alarm when they found themselves suddenly surrounded by the legionaries brandishing short swords and long poles adorned with eagles.

In 1963 a girls' school moved in to Walton Hall. Showing the principal round (prior to an agreement) Lady Hamilton found bundles of eighteenth-century letters in the muniment room. These letters formed the basis of her book *The Mordaunts—an 18th Century Family*, published in 1965, which has the quality of the famous Paston Letters and Celia Fiennes' Diary. It gives delightful glimpses of Walton and its people, including a butler 'whose secret recipe for brewing beer went with him to the grave'.

The Mordaunts were preoccupied with health matters in their correspondence like the colds Sir John always caught when visiting Charlecote, while his wife, Penelope, arranged for Queen Anne to touch the daughter of 'Savidge, a tailor who had come up from Warwickshire' as a cure for the girl's scrofula, the 'King's Evil'.

The Mordaunts were placid Parliamentarians. Sir Charles, the 6th Baronet, might have had employment under the Crown, but was content to seek promotion for his son, John, who became Groom of the Bedchamber to George III. Sir Charles, the 8th Baronet, was in Dublin with the Warwickshire Militia 'looked up to as the finest regiment in Ireland', and saw service chasing Humbert's invading Frenchmen and the Irish rebels when they surrendered at Castlebar in 1789. It is, however, the domestic scene which emerges mainly from the letters—with Walton Hall supplying the Mordaunts' London household with such things as 'consignments of hog's pudding and chine'. Marianne, widow of the 8th Baronet, summed up life at Walton as the nineteenth century dawned: 'I thoroughly enjoyed this summer the beauty, coolness, and comfort of the place and house, drew a good deal in the woods, and felt the luxury of living in such a library.'

The Mordaunt motto, *'Ferro comite'* translates as 'My companion the sword', and insofar as the escutcheons in the windows of Gilbert Scott's marbled entrance hall trace back descent—somewhat obliquely—to the Conquest, perhaps a sword was appropriate, but later Mordaunts turned it into a ploughshare, or maybe a shepherd's crook, in the smiling Dene valley before the Second World War brought back the sword for a while.

At Wellesbourne the Dene divides Wellesbourne Mountford from Wellesbourne Hastings, the Mountfords and the Hastings being influential Midland families of the Middle Ages. Today Wellesbourne is thought of as one picturesque village with several noteworthy pubs.

The club room of the thatched black and white 'Stag's Head' had been booked for a meeting on 7 February 1872, but so many attended that they had to move into the open air beneath the chestnut tree across the road. Lanterns hung from the branches; others were held high on beanpoles, for an opponent of the meeting had switched off the gas lamps and the night was pitch dark. A pig-killing stool was found for the speaker, and from it he urged an audience loosely estimated from 500 to 2,000 to form a trade union and to press for a daily increase of sixpence on their weekly wage of 10s., and a cut in hours to nine per day. The speaker was Joseph Arch of nearby Barford, and this meeting was the inspiration for the ultimate formation of the National Agricultural Labourers' Union.

Arch was born in 1826 at a tiny cottage almost opposite Barford Church, and died there aged 92 in 1919. He began work aged nine earning fourpence a day as a bird-scarer. Ploughboy at 3s. a week; stable boy at 8s; Joseph was earning 11s. weekly when he married. The need for more money when children were born caused him to become a free-lance—gravel digging in Warwick, wood-cutting at Bishop's Tachbrook, then as a hedger, at which he became so proficient that he is described as 'one-time champion hedge-cutter of England' on a memorial bus shelter near a chestnut tree which has replaced the one beneath which he held his first meeting. Soon he was earning up to 3s. 6d. a day.

One item of Joseph's equipment as a trade union leader, public speaking, was nurtured as a Primitive Methodist local preacher, when he advocated also the teetotalism from which he fell so sadly away later. In the 1868 General Election he spoke and voted Liberal.

The immediate outcome of the February meeting was the founding of a Warwickshire Union of farm workers. Committee meetings were held in John Lewis's stone-flagged cottage at Wellesbourne, the funds being kept in two large teacups. At Ratley, Napton, and

16　*Built in 1632, Chesterton Windmill has been restored recently*

17 Charlecote, a Tudor gem, where the Dene runs down to the Avon

18 Compton Verney stands in grounds laid out by 'Capability' Brown

Flecknoe the agricultural workers were stirring. A radical-minded Coventry auctioneer, William Taunton, held a meeting at Stoneleigh and urged farm labourers to organise. Two members of Leamington Trades Council addressed a meeting of 500 at Whitnash, one of them, Henry Taylor, a carpenter, becoming general secretary of the National Agricultural Labourers' Union on its eventual formation. Militancy began. Claims for better pay and conditions were sent, respectfully enough, to landowners such as Sir Charles Mordaunt, with threats of a strike if need be.

This South Warwickshire Strike began when the strikers' organisation had only 5s. in hand, but with 1s. per week impost on farm workers not affected, together with financial help from a public less antipathetic to trade unions and strikes than it is today, it was possible to pay strike benefit of 9s. per week. The farmers, naturally, took up the cudgels, and there were lockouts at Wasperton, Tysoe, and Claverdon. Victimization soon became an instrument of union policy, and at Kineton Petty Sessions John England got three months for 'compelling' Thomas Barnes to leave his employment. But a wage increase from Sir Charles Mordaunt helped end the strike together with strikers leaving for employment in a Liverpool soap factory, on Gateshead dockyards, at Huddersfield waterworks, and as drivers and horsekeepers for the North Eastern Railway. Some even emigrated, and 'migration' expenses cost the Warwickshire Union £112 and strike relief £214, but the union finished the strike with £400 in hand.

On 10 April 1872, in the Primitive Methodist Chapel, Wellesbourne, Arch and others first considered the formation of a national union. This came to fruition on 29 May 1072, at a conference in Leamington, Arch being appointed full-time president of the National Agricultural Labourers' Union at £2 a week. Thereafter this bearded Warwickshire Cincinnatus in the moleskin trousers moved on to a national stage. In 1885 he was elected Liberal M.P. for North-west Norfolk, the first farm labourer to enter Parliament, and numbering among those he represented, as he often proudly said, the Prince of Wales at Sandringham. Before leaving the Commons finally in 1900 Arch became a loyal Liberal Party satellite, 'drinking his bottle of whisky a day but hardly opening his mouth for any other purpose.' In October 1896, the N.A.L.U., whose membership had been steadily falling, was dissolved, and Joseph Arch lost his only income, his salary of between £4 and £5 a week. Friends in the Liberal Party collected £1,200 and bought him a £157 annuity. He became disillusioned with his career as a union leader, and took no interest in the establishment in 1906 of the National Union of Agricultural Workers, which was to honour him in 1922 with an obelisk at his resting place in Barford churchyard.

In 1960 the 'Red Lion' at Barford changed its name to the 'Joseph Arch', the sign depicting him as a mutton-chopped yeoman.

Another Barford inn has an association with Wellesbourne, the 'Granville Arms', named after a family which lived at Wellesbourne Hall, a beautiful William and Mary mansion which still retains its own ice-house. The hall must not be confused with Wellesbourne House, which resembles a home from the American Deep South, though it is now a rubber and plastics factory. Wellesbourne House was built by William Mackay Low, an American millionaire. He is said, as a baby during the Civil War, to have been hidden for safety among the sugar canes by two negro slaves, one of whom eventually accompanied him to Wellesbourne as his cook. Edward VII, a frequent visitor to Wellesbourne House, was said to be very partial to the negro's dishes.

Visitors entering Wellesbourne from Barford often pull up in surprise at the 'Giraffe in the Ash Tree', the most striking memorial of several to Charles Bettridge, blacksmith and agricultural impliment maker, who died in 1971 aged 88. Looking at an angle of the ash tree from his bungalow window, Mr. Bettridge saw in his mind's eye a giraffe, and it took only the addition of a head and two front legs, with a coat of yellow paint copiously spotted black to create the giraffe. This sturdy village character has also left behind the fascinating Bettridge Collection of wooden working models and replicas of buildings, and he is further remembered by Bettridge Place in Wellesbourne. His family first set up as coach-builders 300 years ago in the barn which now has a pheasant windvane at the Malthouse.

Charles Bettridge once told me of shin-kicking contests and dog fights at the 'rat pit' in the 'King's Head', Wellesbourne, which has recently lost its well-known sign of an unidentified king's head raised on a post above four foxes' heads, an indication that the hotel was once the headquarters of the Warwickshire Hunt, from which foxes were chased to north, south, east and west. The Talbot Hotel, nearby, still has its sign of the talbot hound, the crest of the Earls of Shrewsbury.

North of Wellesbourne the Dene enters the Charlecote domain of the Lucys, famous for the conjectural episode of Shakespeare's deer-poaching. Whatever happened between Sir Thomas Lucy (1551-1600) and the playwright, we do know that Shakespeare lampooned him as Justice Shallow in *The Merry Wives of Windsor* and the Second Part of *King Henry IV*, and became a friend of his grandson, Sir Thomas, who succeeded to Charlecote in 1605. The deer continue to attract the crowds to Charlecote today, and the house, given to the National Trust by Sir Montgomerie Fairfax-Lucy in 1945, is popular and rewarding as stately homes go.

Two families which crossed to Hastings with the Conqueror married together and formed the Lucy line which has endured to the twentieth century. Walter de Montfort, of the family which settled at Beaudesert, Henley-in-Arden, married in 1189 an heiress of the Lucy family which had originated at Luce-sur-Orne in Normandy. They set up residence in a manor house which stood to south-eastward of the site of the present hall, and Charlecote passed in direct male descent through the Lucys until 1787.

Spencer Lucy, the eldest son of Shakespeare's friend, who inherited Charlecote, was in Nottingham at the raising of the standard by Charles I, and his two younger brothers died fighting for the king. Another brother, Richard, M.P. for Warwick, had sufficient status with Parliament to prevent Cromwellian resentment falling upon Charlecote. He became one of the 139 'ideally qualified' M.P s forming the Barebones Parliament in 1653.

Charlecote is an architecturally charming place. An Elizabethan gatehouse flanked by polygonal turrets with ogee-shaped caps leads to a hall which might also be Tudor, but which is, in fact, largely nineteenth century. The park was designed by 'Capability' Brown during the 42-year reign at Charlecote of George Lucy, whose funeral in 1786 was so magnificent that the Charlecote deer stampeded into the flooded river, 30 being drowned. George was succeeded by the Rev. John Hammond, his secretary, whose grandmother was a Lucy. Hammond took the name of Lucy along with the family livings of Charlecote and Hampton Lucy, which passed in 1823 to his son, also the Rev. John Lucy, who demolished Hampton Lucy Church and employed Thomas Rickman and Hutchinson to build the present striking Gothic structure with its lofty tower and tall pinnacles.

Charlecote Church was rebuilt about the same time, and is well worth examination. Among its Lucy memorials, that to Shakespeare's friend, Sir Thomas, is of particular interest, showing him mounted on a horse, and incorporating a collection of books in marble. A two-light window in the north wall has a border of fishes—pike, or in their old-fashioned name, lucies. A window nearby is a saint-spotter's gem—St. Leonard, patron of prisoners, with his fetters, and St. Hubert, patron of huntsmen, confronted by a stag with a crucifix between its antlers, in memory of Henry Spencer Leven who died on St. Leonard's Day, 1890. The crossed foxes featured about the church are the device of the Williams of Bodelwyddan, Flintshire, the family of Mary Elizabeth Lucy who rebuilt the church.

The hyphen is prolific in the Lucy name today, the present and fifth baronet being Sir Brian Fulke Cameron-Ramsay-Fairfax-Lucy.

The best viewpoint into the Dene valley around Walton is New-bold Pacey churchyard, from whence the wellingtonias in Spetchley Drive look like a coven of witches. Newbold Pacey Church has a tablet with a memorable verse to a vicar who was a nephew of Robert Southey, the poet, and a more elaborate memorial to Edward Carew and his baby daughter, Felicia 'who died in the 13th day of her age'.

If ever I have to show Warwickshire at its most felicitous to a visitor I take him the half-mile stroll from Ashorne to Newbold Pacey Church. We set out across the cricket pitch, probably unique in that the batsman, walking between the wicket and the pavilion, has to cross a stream by a bridge. The cricket ground skirts Ashorne Manor, where, cemented into a south-facing red brick garden wall above a flower bed, and quite legible from the railings, are nine stones with epitaphs to dogs of the manor. Noodle's verse is heart-catching; Tinker's brings a smile in its last couplet:

> *Mourned by friends in many a sphere;*
> *Only the cats withhold a tear.*

Beyond the cricket ground and across the stream the church is reached by a footpath at the edge of a cornfield and beneath massive elms of Newbold Pacey Manor parkland. It is all an exquisite glimpse of the essential more-leisured England of an earlier day. From Newbold Pacey a track runs westward across the fields to the Ministry of Agriculture Vegetable Research Station, and a couple of miles north, in a loop of the Avon, Westham House offers a charming environment as an adult residential college devoted to countryside and cultural themes—and to Shakespeare. Across the river rises the spire of Sherbourne Church, and in its shadow rests one Harriett Waterloo Grice, born—yes, you've guessed—on 18 June 1815.

In Act I Scene II of *Henry V* Shakespeare has an ambassador of France bring a gift of tennis balls from the Dauphin to King Henry, who says:

> *When we have matched our rackets to these balls,*
> *We will, in France, by God's grace, play a set*
> *Shall strike his father's crown into the hazard.*

The tennis thus referred to, with hazards in the court, is Real or Royal Tennis, an earlier form of the game, played indoors where the ball is allowed to bounce off walls still in play. Such a court, built in Edwardian days, serves the Moreton Morrell Tennis Court Club, between Newbold Pacey and Kineton, which, with a select membership of 165 or so, launched an appeal in 1971 for £40,000 to save the enormous building which houses the court. Warwickshire can claim to have given birth—in 1872—to the first lawn tennis club in the world, at the Manor House Hotel, Leamington Spa. Fifteen years earlier two of the founders had played the first-ever game of lawn tennis, at 'Fairlight', Ampton Road, Edgbaston, Birmingham, their names being Major T. H. Gem and Mr. J. B. Perera.

East of Moreton Morrell the Fosse Way offered good pickings to highwaymen, and one Bendigo Mitchell had his territory hereabouts, ranging north and south of Harwoods House. In a fine old barn at Wiggerland Wood Farm, nearby, I was shown a double gibbet cut in a beam with the inscription 'E. L. 1772, April 14', and told that it commemorated the hanging of two men on Gallows Hill, outside Warwick. Bendigo is said often to have slept in the

'Old Inn', now a private house, at Bishop's Tachbrook, in which village Walter Savage Landor, the poet, lived when a boy, members of his family being buried there. The wife of Charles Kingsley, author of *Westward Ho!*, also lived at The Grove, Bishop's Tachbrook, and though she is buried in Hampshire she has left as her Warwickshire memorial the east window of Bishop's Tachbrook Church.

Approaching Leamington from Bishop's Tachbrook it is worth a short detour to visit Whitnash Church where human mortality is poignantly portrayed in a plaque which reads: 'Friendly regard has inscribed this marble in memory of a family now totally extinct.' The family was that of the Rev. Thomas Morse, who died in 1784, aged 84, and his wife. They had four sons and three daughters, all of whom died without issue. A lighter note is struck in St. John the Baptist's Church, Tachbrook Street, as you enter Leamington. Twenty lancet windows each have one saint, and the only non-British one among them is—St. George, patron saint of England.

CHAPTER SIX

Leamington Spa and its River

Raindrops falling along a three-mile stretch of the Northampton-shire uplands near the Warwickshire border could find themselves flowing down any one of three rivers to widely-separated estuaries. The northernmost would flow via the Nene to the Wash, the southernmost via the Cherwell and Thames to the sea beyond London; while those falling half way between, in a pool below Hellidon windmill, would swell the Leam on its 25-mile course to the Avon, the Severn, and the Bristol Channel.

After three miles in Northamptonshire, a mile west of Staverton the Leam becomes the boundary between Northamptonshire and Warwickshire for three more meandering miles across remote pastures near the canal junction of Braunston to the lost village of Wolfhampcote. Here the river curves round some grassy mounds, the remains of a medieval village abandoned in the late fifteenth century, when sheep-grazing took the place of the arable farming which had employed more hands. A Medieval Village Research Group financed by the city museums of Birmingham and Coventry excavated the site in 1955 and found more than 2,000 items of pottery, broken knives, and buckles, mainly from the early Middle Ages, and a barrel padlock, one of only four ever found in Britain of a type brought over by the Vikings. Some Saxon pottery established that Wolfhampcote was inhabited long before the Norman Conquest.

One of the lords of the manor of Wolfhampcote was Sir Christopher Hatton, to whom it was granted by Queen Elizabeth I. Rumour had it that Hatton was the queen's paramour, and Mary, Queen of Scots, actually taxed her with it. Their relations were extremely friendly, Hatton writing in extravagent terms from the Continent: 'Bear with me, my most dear sweet lady. Passion over-cometh me. Love me, for I love you.' Elizabeth reciprocated to the extent of addressing Hatton as 'My mutton' and 'My bellwether'.

Only the manor house and St. Peter's Church survive at Wolf-hampcote, the latter deserted and with windows broken. It once served three neighbouring hamlets, Flecknoe, Nethercote, and Saw-bridge. Flecknoe still has its stocks outside the Post Office, and an inn with the unusual name of the Old Olive Bush. At Sawbridge, some years ago, an old inhabitant laughing scornfully at modern ideas of building prefabrication, showed me inside a fine barn where the timbers' ends were numbered with roughly-cut Roman numerals showing what dovetailed into what—a system which can be seen in many old timbered buildings.

That these border uplands are spacious and deserted was proved once when I walked across them to Priors Marston, calf-deep in snow on the higher fields and ankle-deep in mud at lower gates. Present-ing myself the worse for wear at Priory Farm, I was greeted with amazement.

'Has your aircraft crashed up on the fields?' the farmer's wife asked me.

Priors Marston and Priors Hardwick, two miles distant, get their names from having belonged to the monks of Coventry Priory. At Priory Farm one of the fields, now known as 'Bury Yard', was once a monks' graveyard, and I heard rumours of a tunnel from the farm running to Catesby Church, two and a half miles distant. If I be-lieved only a quarter of the stories I hear of secret tunnels I should be afraid of sudden subsidence wherever I go.

The products of a village craft at Priors Marston, now in the third generation of craftsmen, have gone far and wide. These are the Gimson chairs associated with the name of the late Edward Gardiner. While he turned and fashioned the legs and backs of the chairs, Victor Neal fashioned their rush bottoms from native and imported Dutch rushes. Mr. Gardiner's assistant was Mr. Neal's son, Neville, who continues making the chairs while his son, Lawrence, does the rush-bottoming.

Back to the River Leam which has taken a westward turn near Wolfhampcote towards Grandborough, running south of Willoughby where the church, dedicated to St. Nicholas, does him proud in the east window. A patron saint of sailors, he is depicted as Bishop of Myra with a ship bearing on its sail a picture of the three children he saved from a frying vat in which an innkeeper proposed preparing them as dinner for the bishop and his retinue. A girl stands beside Nicholas, for is he not also patron saint of children? Also in the window are the three money bags in which the saint delivered gifts of gold to a poor Christian man as dowries for his daughters, thus making him the original Santa Claus. The church has a wall memorial to George Watson, a naval captain who died on the Guinea coast in 1674, leaving a legacy for the poor of Willoughby. His epitaph reads:

> *Death hath controuled a Captain bold,*
> *Yet loss of life is gain;*
> *Especially when charity*
> *For ever doth remaine.*

Swollen by the Rains Brook coming down from Rugby way, the Leam flows peacefully to Grandborough Mill where there is an eel trap beside the sluice gate. The river wakes to thunder down a weir into a deep pool where large pike have been caught beside Mill House with its kitchen where the wheel once turned, though it is half a century since Grandborough Mill was worked. Grandborough's inn is the 'Shoulder of Mutton', but opposite the church with its avenue of limes a cottage bears a name which speaks of past licensed conviviality, the 'Royal George Inn'. Nearby at Woolscott, 'Harrow House', once the 'Old Harrow Inn', sets one wondering why, with so many Ploughs, the Harrow should be so rare a name for an inn.

Thurlaston Bridge, which carries the Dunchurch-Southam road across the Leam at Kites Hardwick, replaces one which was destroyed during the Great Civil War 'for the safety of the county', though in 1648 the county had to pay £16 for its repair.

The village of Leamington Hastings marks a half-way point along the river both physically and phonetically. Upstream the pronunciation is 'Leem'; downstream it becomes 'Lem'—the Hastings derives from the Hastang family, medieval lords of the manor. A squat row of cream-coloured almshouses in Leamington Hastings was founded by Humphrey Davies who, on his death in 1607, gave his lands stretching some miles downstream for the maintenance of them. Something went wrong with his bequest for, according to a tablet on the almshouses 'they were detayned for 26 years' to be 'recovered by the help of Sir Thomas Trevor' in 1633.

Birdingbury Hall gives the Leam possibly its most gracious building. With it, above the river valley, St. Leonard's church tower is a small replica of St. Paul's, London, but for its domestic chimney. The Rev. Henry Homer, a vicar of Birdingbury who died in 1791, provided his own congregation with his 17 children. He was something of a transport historian, writing about rivers, canals, and roads. At Marton, two miles west of Birdingbury, the Leam flows beneath a successor to the bridge built by John Middleton in the fifteenth century to save the villagers paying tolls on the bridge downstream at Eathorpe on the Roman Fosse Way. Below the tower of the Church of St. Espirt, the little River Itchen, coming up from the south, joins the Leam as it loops round Eathorpe Park.

In my wanderings I am always interested in builders' initials and dates on houses. Often the initials are those of obscure people, and walking into Eathorpe for the first time I noticed several cottages with the initial S.S. and the date 1862. The same initials and date appeared on the bridge across the Leam, where I leaned on the parapet and watched large chub in a pool underneath the weir. An enquiry led me to Poplar Farm, and I learned that the initials were those of Samuel Shepheard, and that the builder of the bridge at Eathorpe was the same Samuel Shepheard who, around 1850, built the original Shepheard's Hotel in Cairo, probably the most famous hotel the world has ever known. Frequently featured in exotic films and books before the Second World War, it was burned down by an Egyptian mob in 1952, though another hotel has risen on the site. The visitors' book at Shepheard's Hotel held so valuable a collection of celebrities' signatures that it was kept chained down. A 100-years-old, account of the arrival of the overland transit from India at Shepheard's says: 'When the vans of the transit lumbered to the door at Shepheard's in the early dawn, dire was the confusion that ensued as passengers poured into the passages in search of food and sleeping accommodation. In they swarmed, men in pith helmets and women in indescribable costumes, to take forcible possession of any rooms that might seem to be vacant in advance of their competitors without asking any questions of the landlord or his clerks.'

Samuel Shepheard was born in Little Preston Manor, near Daventry, in 1816; his parents died young, and he was brought up by an uncle at the 'Crown Inn', Leamington and apprenticed to a pastry cook. He disliked the discipline and ran away to sea to become an officer steward in a liner. Still he bridled against authority, so when he sided with some mutineers he was put ashore in Egypt with only a shilling in his pocket. He found a job in the British Hotel, Cairo, prospered, became manager, was befriended by Abbas Pasha, and built his own hotel. Then came good luck in the form of the Crimean War and the Indian Mutiny, from each of which Shepheard got what he described as 'good pickings' as officers and their families in transit stayed at Shepheard's Hotel.

He sold out in 1860 and went to Eathorpe Hall as squire, building the bridge because his carriage often stuck in the ford. At Poplar Farm I was shown the current minute book of Eathorpe Parish Council, an enormous volume over a century in use, the first entry being signed on 25 April 1862 by Shepheard, then chairman. His signature continued until 29 March 1866, when it was becoming shaky. He died not three months later, on 12 June, aged only 50, and this one-time Middle Eastern potentate is buried with his wife beneath a humble cross in Wappenbury churchyard across the river from the hall where he spent his last years. With Samuel Shepheard at Wappenbury lie the sixth Earl of Clonmel and Frank Henry Bluemel, founder of the cycle pump firm.

An Iron Age earthwork much damaged by ploughing and natural erosion surrounds Wappenbury, and excavations through sections of it by the Coventry and District Archaeological Society have disclosed pottery of the Romano-British period together with remains of four kilns. The investigations came about as the result of a survey of the Leam valley which proved that it 'was heavily settled during at least the third and fourth centuries.'

Chapels of ease were often built in medieval days because of the dangerous access through floods to the mother church. In the thirteenth century Sir Geoffrey de Corbicum, lord of the manor of Wappenbury, established a priest at Hunningham across the Leam to obviate this danger. There today, a pleasant field walk from Wappenbury, with a footbridge crossing of the river where chub can often be seen cruising, stands St. Margaret's Church with a lilliputian weatherboarded bell turret.

Offchurch, just downstream, gets its name from Offa, King of Mercia, who died in 796, and is sometimes said to be buried there. It is claimed, too, that a chapel on the Ouse near Bedford has his bones, but the certain place of his burial is not known. The church at Offchurch, which has a double-decker pulpit, is largely Norman, the stonework round one of its windows being decorated with a charming little snake, first cousin to one at Stoneleigh, near Kenilworth. The dedication at Offchurch is to St. Gregory, the Pope of '*non Angli sed angeli*' fame, and the Stag's Head of the village inn comes from the crest of the Knightley family, long resident at Offchurch Bury, a stone Tudor house with more recent additions. While the Leam loops round Offchurch Bury, a pleasant right of way takes the walker through the park to Holly Walk, Leamington Spa, by-passing the village of Radford Semele, named after a Norman family from Semilly which held the manor of Radford in the reign of Henry I.

At Newbold Comyn the Leam enters Leamington Spa through land long in the hands of the Willes family, which gave its name and crest to the bridge in Willes Road. There was a mill at Newbold Comyn when Domesday Book was compiled, and another on the site of what became Oldham's Mill, where John Oldham built a boathouse and pioneered boating on the Leam just over a century ago. Leamington's principal bridge, the Victoria bridge, had its foundation stone laid in 1840 by Dr. Henry Jephson. Beneath it, and alongside the Pump Room Gardens to the Adelaide Bridge, rebuilt in 1891, the Leam flows by leafy ways to join the Avon just downstream of Portobello Bridge at Emscote, named after the Spanish base in the West Indies captured by Admiral 'Grog' Vernon in 1739 during the War of Jenkins' Ear. Portobello became a popular name for inns, and one stood on the Warwick side of the bridge until recently, the name being perpetuated in the Portobello Works of Thomas Potterton Ltd., and in their social club on the site of the old inn.

All Saints, Leamington's parish church, has a tower 145 feet tall, built as recently as 1901-2, a splendid vantage point to look at a town which has grown from a village of 300 inhabitants in 1800 to a royal spa with a population of nearly 50,000. The tower itself constitutes a major climbing problem, an initial grope up a winding stone turret followed by a series of wooden ladders passing through a ringing chamber and another bare floor to a weirdly spacious gloom where a steep ladder alongside one wall leads to a wooden platform along the next, and so to a last long ladder up a third wall giving access to the roof through a trapdoor.

Beneath the tower in the churchyard, their memorials already decaying, lie two men who were largely responsible for Leamington's mushroom growth. This originated from the development of seven saline springs with curative properties, waters of the muriated sulphate character with a large percentage of lime salts. William Abbotts, landlord of the Black Dog Inn, established the first baths in the 1780s. Benjamin Satchwell, postmaster, shoemaker, poet, and founder of the Leamington Spa Charity which became Warneford Hospital, was commemorated on an inscription in Aylesford's Free Well, almost beneath the tower. This read: 'Ye who drink of these waters remember Benjamin Satchwell who in 1784 discovered and proclaimed the health-giving virtues of this spring'. The inscription was destroyed when the well house was demolished in 1961, though a memorial stone still marks the position. One of my abiding memories is the clangour of the chained metal cup dropped against the fountain in the well house whenever I visited relatives in Leamington during my Warwick childhood.

More saline springs were discovered. On a map of Leamington in 1818 Lillington Lane, where Satchwell and Abbotts had first seen the bubbles in a ditch which led them to discover a second spring, had become Bath Street, and in addition to the Pump Room and Aylesford's Well; Robins's, Wise's, Read's, and Smart's baths spoke of a spa development which was causing Cheltenham and Bath to look to their laurels as invalids and others flocked to Leamington Spa to take the waters.

From the vantage point of All Saints' tower one is at once attracted to the view westward by the more slender tower of St. Mary's, rising over a compact assembly of roofs at Warwick two miles away. Much nearer, to the south, a red line of buses, and black metals running into the railway station draw the eye to Leamington's transport centre. Beyond it, off Tachbrook Road, the newish Shrubland Estate provides homes for workers at the Lockheed factory. On this spot once stood the residence of Matthew Wise who, in 1790, founded Wise's, later Curtis's, Baths, which were demolished in 1850 to make way for the Leamington-Rugby railway line. Directly he leaves the station the visitor gets a preview, in the Great Western and Crown Hotels, of the wrought-iron balconies which date Leamington as a Regency growth. A left turn beneath the railway into Bath Street, and a half-mile walk towards and up The Parade, reveals Leamington as a true child of its period with balconies, porticoes, and pediments galore, though a supermarket has taken the place of the old 'Parthenon', opposite Regent Place, where Robert Elliston lost a fortune with his magnificent assembly rooms, ballroom, and library.

A few more yards, and practically at the foot of the tower lies the essential heart of Leamington—Victoria Bridge, with the Loft Theatre, phoenix-like after two fires, up the colonnade beside the leafy Leam, The Royal Pump Room and Baths, and the entrance to the Pump Room Gardens and the Jephson Gardens, the latter bringing Bournemouth to Warwickshire with their flowers, lawns, and fountains where rainbows glisten in the sunshine and peace and warmth descend like a benediction. Looking much like the Duke of Windsor, Dr. Henry Jephson stands in the Greek Temple in the gardens which recall his successful treatment of spa patients in the mid-nineteenth century, when the ailing aristocracy flocked to Leamington to lose their gout and to have their visits perpetuated in a snobs' gallery of street names. This up-and-coming town was obviously a hopeful spot for a young doctor, and having received his diploma in 1819 Dr. Jephson first came to Leamington. Born at Sutton-in-Ashfield, Nottinghamshire, in 1798, Jephson as a young man lost two fingers of his right hand in a laboratory explosion. He went to Leamington as assistant to Dr. Chambers in Union Parade, became his partner, and married a Yorkshire girl. On Chambers' retirement in 1826 Jephson carried on the practice for a few months before going to Glasgow. He returned to Leamington in 1828, but soon moved on to Cheltenham.

The Jephson legend had begun in Leamington however, and many residents petitioned him to return. This he did, setting up his plate at 7, York Terrace. With a rapid increase in his practice he built a fine house in Warwick Street—Beech Lawn, which he made his home in 1831—on the site now occupied by the Warwick County

Fire Brigade headquarters. The growing Leamington of the day did honour to royalty and the visiting aristocracy in its street names— Gordon Street, Bedford Street, Somers Place, and many more. Meanwhile the aristocracy, and even royalty, were consulting Jephson, so that for some years his annual professional income was little short of £25,000. By 1845 a move was afoot in the town, now a royal borough, to honour Dr. Jephson 'in recognition of the advantages Leamington had derived from his enlightened practice'. Lord Somerville presided over a committee soliciting funds for the purpose, and at each meeting some entertainment was added to the business. Thus one day we find a Mr. Baker entertaining the committee with a song to the tune of 'The Warwickshire Lads and Lasses'. One of the verses ran:

> Our Jephson compared is to no man,
> To Frenchmen, nor Grecian, nor Roman;
> His head and his heart have the same noble span,
> And the Man of all Men is our Leamington Man.

The committee's ultimate decision was to acquire the Newbold Gardens for the public and to rename them the Jephson Gardens. They were made up to 14 acres by land belonging to the Willes family, stretching either side of a path leading from the Willes residence to the west lodge opposite the Pump Rooms. Early last century a tenant of this pasture was a burly Farmer Court who rode around on a plump cob discouraging trespassing boys. Court's successor, Jackson, had laid out the area as a pleasure garden in 1834, and to help him sell plots for building in what is now Newbold Terrace, Squire Willes determined that the gardens should never be built on, and that residents in the villas rising along the terrace would have perpetual free admission. To these gardens the committee obtained a lease for 2,000 years at £30 annual rental, and a statue would complete Leamington's tribute to Dr. Jephson. So Baker sang a new verse:

> A statue is very inviting,
> One to Jephson we all take delight in;
> This task to complete be Hollins's still,
> For the Skill of all Skill is our Warwickshire Skill....

Peter Hollins, a Birmingham sculptor, was commissioned to do the statue. Writing Lord Somerville that his usual charge for a statue in Carrara marble seven feet tall was £1,000 with £100 for a pedestal in Sicilian marble and extra for fixing the statue, Hollins nevertheless offered to do the job for £1,000 all in, 'because of the beneficial effect it cannot fail to produce on my future professional career'. The statue was inaugurated on 29 May 1849, an occasion saddened by the blindness which had come upon Jephson in 1847, an affliction which ended his career as a doctor though not his public life, for he became an elected member of Leamington's first local board in 1852, and in 1860 chairman of the company which bought the Pump Rooms from the Hon. Charles Bertie Percy of Guy's Cliff. He died on 14 May 1878, and lies beside his wife in Old Milverton Cemetery.

The naming of Jephson Gardens sparked off a feud between Leamington Corporation and the Willes family, squires of Newbold Comyn, half a mile upstream of Adelaide Bridge on the Leam. It was Edward Willes who, in 1846, gave Newbold meadows to Leamington, and he took umbrage when the public gardens on the site were named after Dr. Jephson. The Willes family would have preferred Newbold Gardens, or even Willes Gardens, and these feelings were aggravated when the Corporation waited 28 years after the donor's death before raising an obelisk to him in Jephson Gardens. The ill-feeling lay dormant, only to flare around 1950 when the Corporation gave notice of entry to Welch's Meadow, across the Leam from the Willes home, to take test borings for a reservoir. Squire William Willes was riparian owner of both banks of the Leam, which gave him rights over the river, so, as the Corporation's three-year boating lease had just expired he refused to renew it. For ten years boating was banned between the weir and Offchurch until in 1960 Mr. Edward Willes opened the river again.

The Spa itself, financed partly by the Regional Hospital Board and Leamington Corporation, still gives 40,000 treatments annually, mostly in hydro-therapy, and almost all under National Health. The Pump Room Restaurant is open daily, and with an orchestra on Sundays, except in winter, it offers a nostalgic escape back to yesteryear. A new Royal Spa Centre, opened in June 1972, in Newbold Terrace with a hall seating 850 and a lecture theatre. Over 400 Leamington

19   *The tomb in Charlecote Church of Sir Thomas Lucy, died 1605, son of the Sir Thomas whose deer Shakespeare is supposed to have poached*

properties are designated as of architectural and historical interest, and the survival of some of Regency Leamington is assured with the Corporation's renovation of Landsdowne Crescent and Clarendon Square, though the bath chair colonel of Edwardian days would be shattered by the takeover of the public seats in the Pump Room and Jephson Gardens by the borough's large Asian population. These are the new workers at Automotive Products, making car components, the Ford foundry making agricultural implements, and Flavels, manufacturers of cookers, Leamington's main sources of employment, along with smaller firms on the new industrial estates.

South of the River Leam the Warwick and Napton section of the Grand Union Canal strikes more directly than the river back to the Northamptonshire border, assuming a peculiar creamy-brown muddy appearance in the Lower Lias after leaving the Keuper Marl around Long Itchington. In fact a canalside inn at Stockton Locks, a mile or so east of Long Itchington is called the 'Blue Lias', and blazons on its sign a dinosaur, the dominant life form 180 million years ago when the Lower Lias was deposited. Less recognizably palaeontological is the Cuttle Inn which faces the Two Boats Inn across the canal at Long Itchington. The bulletlike belemnite, a prolific fossil of the Lias, derives from a prehistoric cuttle fish.

The Grand Union Canal Company was formed in 1929, an amalgamation of eight canals of which Warwickshire contributed the Warwick and Birmingham, opened in 1793, and the Warwick and Napton, 1794. These waterways retained a busy commerce between Birmingham and London up to the 1950s, the main, strangely assorted, cargoes being metal ingots and tomato puree. As recently as 1967 I travelled with a pair of narrow-boats, *Bunstead* and its butty, from the Rugby Portland Cement Works near Southam to Bordesley Wharf, Birmingham. This was probably the last pair on a once-thriving waterway, worked by Chris Jones, born on the Shropshire Union Canal, near Wolverhampton, and his wife, Violet, also born on a boat, at Long Itchington. Fellows, Morton, and Clayton owned most of the boats on the Grand Union early this century, though the cement and lime works of Charles Nelson at Stockton and Kaye at Long Itchington operated their own fleets. Today only the Southam factory of Rugby Portland Cement Works flaunts the characteristic white plume from its chimney, the Lakin Works at

Harbury having recently closed. Until recent improved techniques in producing cement were evolved the countryside around the works was perpetually obliterated in an off-white frost of dust from the chimneys.

Two miles east of Long Itchington the canal is crossed by the Welsh Road which comes in from the north-west and strikes south-east out of the country, the road by which the Welsh drovers once conducted their cattle to London. South of the canal on this old drovers' road is Bascote Heath, a hamlet memorable for the butterfly orchis and green twayblade growing in Itchington Wood; for a roadside notice: 'Passers by, gipsy and gentry alike, are requested to leave no litter'; and for its tiny graveyard hidden deep among trees. This is a gem. Almost every headstone is of interest, one being inscribed with all 16 lines of Tennyson's 'Crossing the Bar'.

Long Itchington, on the River Itchen, takes pride in being the birthplace of St. Wulstan who, as Bishop of Worcester during the Conquest, discovered the virtues of appeasement, being the only bishop to collaborate with the Normans, thus being enabled to build the first cathedral at Worcester, of which his crypt, in particular, remains. Tall Lombardy poplars surround the village pond at Long Itchington, scene of a tragedy on Sunday, 20 February 1910 when a 23-year-old local preacher, William Herringshaw, sheltering from a thunderstorm beneath a tree was killed by lightning.

At Stockton lives Charles Gardner, to have known whom has been a heart-warming experience in a world where so often true worth reaps no particular reward. Thirty years ago, aged 40, Mr. Gardner had to give up his job at Stockton Cement Works with a suspect heart. He took up wood-turning to make a few Christmas presents, improvising a lathe from an old sewing machine. His interest grew, both in his products and the wood with which he works, and today, nationally famous as a craftsman, he retains that same dual interest. His model fair roundabout interests him more because it embodies 78 varieties of wood than from his own handiwork in its construction. He has met several members of the Royal Family at successive Royal Shows. For the Queen Mother he made a salad bowl from a wellingtonia which grew at Ufton rectory, near Leamington; for the late Princess Royal a fruit bowl from a monkey-puzzle tree growing in Rugby Water Tower Gardens.

He is always on the lookout for new wood—thick rose roots from his own garden, an outsize gooseberry bush at Napton, a lilac from a sister of Lord 'Rab' Butler at Kenilworth. He has used one of Packwood's famous yews. An ilex once blew down at Warwick High School for Girls and he made egg-cups for every girl in the school. Ask Charles Gardner how he enjoyed a holiday in Majorca and he tells you that he brought home some eucalyptus, olive, and locust wood.

A letter signed 'Montgomery of Alamein' commending the fine workmanship of a flat dish occupies pride of place in the visitors' book kept by the Gardners. A quick glance shows entries from Switzerland, Germany, Sweden, Denmark, New Zealand, Botswana, Indonesia, and Nigeria, with the Mayor of Warwick, Rhode Island, for good measure. Mr. Gardner has planted 70 different trees and shrubs in his own garden, including sumachs, Pekin willows, a rowan from Killarney, and a cypress from Bodnant in Wales. In his workshop he will casually pick up an offset of wood and identify it at once—damson, robinia, silver birch, walnut.

Now, without any diminution of his interest in wood-turning, Charles Gardner has begun collecting and renovating gipsy caravans, four of which add colour to his garden, for from his little terrace house in Stockton he has moved to a charming bungalow which he built in spacious grounds—he calls it 'The Arboretum'. In one of his window ledges are small panels of 72 varieties of wood sent by Australian pen-friends who first contacted him after reading an article of mine about his wood-turning.

As the Warwick and Napton Canal approaches its junction with the Oxford Canal, the presiding genius over the countryside is the derelict windmill high on Napton Hill above the brickworks. Such are the windings of the Oxford Canal that it appears bewilderingly first on one hand, then on the other. Napton Church, its windows rich with heraldry, has an incised brass to John Shuckburgh, who died in 1625. His ancestor, an earlier John, married Joan, daughter of Adam Napton, and the Shuckburgh name appears on the map east of Napton on the Daventry road in the village of Lower Shuckburgh, and at Upper Shuckburgh where the family still lives in the hall among the trees, surrounded by 4,000 of their acres.

From the earlier timber-framed Shuckburgh Hall on 22 October

1642 Squire Richard Shuckburgh set out for a day's hunting. To his astonishment, for he knew of no war being fought, he encountered an army led by Charles I who is alleged to have asked him: 'Who is this intent on pleasure while the king fights for his throne?' Shuckburgh returned his hounds to the kennels, aroused his tenantry, and next day fought for Charles at Edgehill and was knighted on the battlefield. Subsequently, Sir Richard, with his third wife, Grace, daughter of Sir Thomas Holte of Aston Hall, Birmingham, fortified Shuckburgh Hill and gallantly opposed the Parliamentary forces before being taken prisoner. He died in 1656, but at the Restoration his eldest son, John, was created a baronet. Today, eleven baronets later, Sir Charles Gerald Stewkley Shuckburgh still lives on Shuckburgh Hill, where vistas between luxuriant trees and across the deer park take in a spacious landscape.

Spotted fallow deer roam the parkland beyond a ha-ha and peacocks strut on close-cut lawns. Inside a hedge of golden yew, Sir George the 9th Baronet, planted out a garden to represent the trenches of the Redan in the Crimea, where he had been decorated by both our French and Turkish allies. He is one of many Shuckburghs commemorated in the church beside the hall—a 'peculiar', under no diocese. Sir Richard, of Edgehill fame, appears there, his features remarkably like those of his king, and surrounded by skulls with a brace of cherubim blowing trumpets. Four fine brasses have been removed from the chancel floor to the greater safety of the walls. Heraldic shields glow from the windows, the arms of noble families with which the Shuckburghs are united, but from this splendid mortuary I emerged smiling at a line in the pompous Georgian recital of the virtues of the fourth baronet: 'He was exactly regular in the duties of his closet'.

Lower Shuckburgh Church in the village is all architecture and nothing else. One row of four houses on the main road bear the initials H.J.S.—of Major Henry James Shuckburgh, who served in the Second Afghan War and has left a quartet of house names as a legacy, Cabul, Nowshera, Joaki, and Gundamuck, where the occupants would prefer a more elegant name.

The Oxford Canal, considered one of the most delectable of inland waterways, half encircles Napton Hill before making its way up five locks to Marston Doles and beyond, where it is pushed into a wide westward detour by Wormleighton Hill before crossing into Oxfordshire through a cutting which was the Fenny Compton Tunnel until 1868 when the roof was removed. Only 30 years ago up to half a dozen boats would tie up for the night at the 'Bull and Butcher', Napton, no longer an inn though the name can be faintly discerned on the wall. Those were the days of famous canal families such as the Hones, and of Joe Skinner of the 'Friendship' pulled by his famous mule.

The rectangle of some 20 square miles of country bounded on the east and south by the Oxford Canal, and on the west and north by main roads radiating from Southam, is the emptiest in Warwickshire. The map shows it crossed only by the narrow Welsh Road with a link to Napton, with few farm names, and only four spinneys. This 'desert' was created by depopulation which began in the mid-fourteenth century when arable was turned to pasture because fewer men were needed to tend sheep than crops. Flat, with a variation of only 150 feet, but for one hill of 454 feet at Ladbroke Hill Farm, it is lonesome walking country with great skyscapes, a primitive tract, a countryside which could have inspired Rudyard Kipling :

> And see you after rain the trace
> Of mound, and ditch, and wall?

History and pre-history can still be traced vividly hereabouts. The fieldpaths were the tracks of the Saxons a thousand and more years ago. A reconstructed plan of Wormleighton village and its approaches in 1200 A.D. looks remarkably like the current one inch map, the Oxford Canal which since 1778 has serpentined around the 400-feet contour being the major addition. A thousand years ago the A423 between Southam and Banbury was already there, called simply The Street. The road from Priors Hardwick to Wormleighton was one of the Ridge Ways, much earlier than Saxon times. Two miles north of Wormleighton, joining these two tracks, ran the Salt Street on its way from Priors Marston to Droitwich.

To the walker who leaves the A423 just south of Ladbroke, the few names on his map were there in some form in Saxon days. Away on his right is Hodnell Manor Farm, originally the hill of the Saxon, Hoda; across the A423, Watergall—poor, damp ground

—and there, too, Chapel Ascote, originally Eadston's Cottage. Near Radbourn a thousand years ago five tracks met at a ford. This village, like Stoneton and others nearby, was depopulated at the end of the fourteenth century, but still the fieldpaths meet there, and the walker continues towards Wormleighton across the Salt-Street and Wilman's Brook by what, in 1200 and earlier, was known as Wilman's Ford.

The earliest known name of Wormleighton was Wilman Lehttune —Wilman's kitchen garden, and at the time of the Saxon settlement the village lay to north of its present site, the tumbled pasture showing the discerning eye just where. Even the less observant cannot fail to see the moated site of the lord of the manor's homestead and the line of four connected stewponds in the open field below the village to the north-west. These led to a large fishpond, now enclosed as a square field.

A track from the fields leads uphill beneath tall trees to Wormleighton Church where two memorials catch the eye. A small slab to Thomas Parker says sombrely: 'To thy reflection mortal friend, the advise of Moses I commend: be wise and meditate thy end.' More elaborate in the chancel is a memorial to John Spencer, heir to Sir Robert Spencer, who 'departed this life at Blois in France the sixth of August after the computation of the Church of England, and the sixteenth after the new computation in the year of our Lord Christ 1610, being 19 years old, 8 monethes, and odd days, never maryed'. This date problem obviously refers to the change made in the Julian Calendar throughout Europe in 1582 when, in order to correct the calendar to leap years, Pope Gregory XIII ordained 5 October to become 15 October, though this change to the Gregorian system was not introduced into England until 1752.

The Spencers were the great family at Wormleighton Manor until they moved across the county boundary to Althorp in Northamptonshire. They have never lost their association with Wormleighton, and Viscount Althorp, heir to the Spencer earldom, is landlord there today. One Spencer divided not only his allegiance but his corpse between Wormleighton and Althorp, for a seventeenth-century round stone in the floor close to the altar rails bears the inscription: 'Here lyeth the bowells of Robert, Lord Spencer.' His body is buried in the family chapel at Brington, Althorp.

Alongside the church Wormleighton Manor seems to be an incomplete grouping of a gatehouse and one wing. There was more, but after being used in 1642 as the headquarters of Prince Rupert before Edgehill it was burned down by the Royalists 'to prevent the Rebells making it a garrison'. Wormleighton Manor was built by John Spencer between 1516 and 1519, when he was knighted. His uncle, also John, was a farmer living at Hodnell who, in 1485, took a hundred-years lease of many acres of land thereabouts from William Catesby. Sir John Spencer had farmed the manor of Snitterfield, near Stratford, but moved to Hodnell on his uncle's death to supervise the extensive grazing business there. Soon he was renting pasture in Wormleighton, Fenny Compton, Ladbroke, and Stoneton, and quick profits from grazing enabled him to buy the manor of Wormleighton outright along with other property, to which, in 1508, he added the manor of Althorp.

By his death in 1522 Sir John had built a 'model village' where Wormleighton now stands. Around it the once open landscape had been enclosed with thick double hedges that still remain, and in the enclosures large flocks of sheep grazed with cattle and horses. In the winter of 1610-11, the first Baron Spencer of Wormleighton received £1,067 for wool and £1,539 for stock. In 1643 the third Baron Spencer was created Earl of Sunderland, and somewhere along that line the Spencer was linked with the Churchill surname of the Dukes of Marlborough, whose coat-of-arms quarters the two frettes and three scallop shells which appear on the interior of the gatehouse at Wormleighton. So this remote Warwickshire village proudly claims a link with Sir Winston Leonard Spencer Churchill.

Though the Spencers chose Althorp as their seat, Wormleighton and its environs bear many marks of their astonishing rise from modest beginnings. The great wool barn through which flowed so much of the family income in the sixteenth century is gone, giving place in 1848 to a group of tall cottages known as the Ten Commandments. The old pinfold or 'stockbank' became a neat stone bus shelter in 1955 with three majestic wellingtonias towering above it. Four farms now operate at Wormleighton, and I was recently invited into Church Farm from which Mr. John Heritage farms 330 acres, to 'see a priest's cupboard'. The exciting recess I was shown gives point to the belief that Church Farm, alongside the gatehouse, was part of the bakehouse and kitchens of the manor house. Mr. Heritage told me: 'The war changed the pattern here. Before it was grassland. Then during the war we had to plough up 80% of the land, and we've gone back only to about 50-50. The arable is mainly wheat with some barley, and I graze black Welsh bullocks and a breeding flock of Suffolk cross sheep. In this heavy clay we must get the arable done by the end of November—it's too heavy to work in the winter rain.'

Mr. Heritage goes to Wales to buy his cattle, thus keeping up the local associations of the Welsh Road.

Back along the Southam road, Ladbroke Church finds no place in any tourist itinerary of Warwickshire, but I find it the most interesting church in the county, a hagiologist's delight because of the saints in its windows. Never mind that the glass is not old—to me the subject matters more. The plan provided names 58 saints in the east window alone, including such rare ones as Lucy holding her eyes on a tray; Ambrose with his beehive; and Sebastian, naked and shot through with arrows. Ss. Agnes and James the Great appear with St. Nicholas in a north nave name window, dedicated in gratitude for their wedding by Lady Agnes Townshend and James Durham. Look carefully for the sign manual of the artist, Webb—a charming little spider's web. The Kempe wheatsheaf sign manual appears in a window with Ss. James the Less and Eunice. Another name window in the chancel has three small pictures of Ss. Edmund, John the Divine, and Wilfred—an intriguing bit of detection this, and who could wish for a better epitaph than that at Ladbroke to Stephen Sprigg: 'Sacred to the memory of a Quiet Life, largely spent in the cultivation of God's beautiful earth'?

Southam, a pleasant little market town with a spacious main street, boasts a mention in Act V Scene I of *Henry VI, Part III.* Warwick the Kingmaker is anxiously awaiting his army before a confrontation with Edward IV at Coventry, and Sir John Somerville tells him that Clarence is not far distant: 'At Southam I did leave him with his forces, and do expect him here some two hours hence'. Southam can dispute the claim of Powick Bridge, near Worcester, to be the first encounter of a later civil war, for in August, 1642, the day after Charles I raised his standard at Nottingham, there was a skirmish lasting four hours at Southam between Parliament forces and Royalists. Charles I slept the night of 21 October 1642, at Southam, two days before the Battle of Edgehill.

Aqueous light from much green glass illumines Southam's wide church with its slender pillars, its rood loft, and angel lectern. There is a tradition of long service here, four Oldhams having been churchwardens between 1844 and 1932, while I recall that in the choir on Good Friday 1956 there were six Rathbones, George, born in 1877, three of his sons, one grandson, and his brother Bill, aged 85. The steeple rises on stepped buttresses across the Leamington road from the Black Dog Inn, where the sign is a mystery—a knight in armour, with another being executed in the background—until you remember that Piers Gaveston, Edward II's favourite, the unfortunate one on the block, used to call the Earl of Warwick the 'Black Dog of Arden'.

Southam once had its hiring fair when agricultural and domestic workers stood in the market with symbols of their jobs, the carters distinguished by whipcord round their hats, thatchers by woven straw, and shepherds by their crooks. Up to 1840 or thereabouts Southam had an annual Lady Godiva procession, headed by 'Old Brazen Face', a man wearing a bull's mask. A traditional Godiva was accompanied by a black woman, and behind them on horseback in a box frame representing a house and windows, rode Peeping Tom. Becoming too bacchanalian the procession was ultimately banned. Today Southam is law-abiding enough, though the wherewithal for liveliness is there in the 'Black Dog', the 'Craven Arms', the 'Red Lion', the 'Crown', the 'Bull', the 'Bowling Green', and the 'Beeswing'. Some have elaborate signs, and there is yet another dignified grey-fronted hostelry calling itself, the 'Old Mint House', where from the fifteenth to the eighteenth century trade tokens were minted in lead, alloys, and leather. A fourteenth-century building, originally linked with one of Coventry's religious houses, the 'Old Mint' serves food and drink in a charming atmosphere of antiques, the Armoury Bar being of absorbing interest to those interested in guns.

Another of Southam's attractions is a zoo just beyond the town on the Daventry road, but for a more indigenous breed than the exotic creatures here we must go three miles north to Hill Farm, Leamington Hastings, where Mr. William E. Nokes is one of possibly two only breeders in the county of Warwickshire Longhorn cattle. The Longhorn, spreading from the north, became very popular in the eighteenth century in Leicestershire, Northamptonshire and Warwickshire, so much so indeed that in the last of these counties it took the name of Warwickshire Longhorn. It grows considerably between two and a half and three years old, attaining a heavy weight yet yielding very lean meat, and it is as pleasing as surprising a sight to encounter on Warwickshire pastures.

CHAPTER SEVEN

Warwick and the Castles

Warwickshire can boast one of the most exquisite views in England, one thought by Sir Walter Scott to be unsurpassed in the Kingdom. This is the magnificent grey wall of Warwick Castle downstream of the Avon bridge, rising in majesty above the tree-fringed river. From beneath Caesar's Tower at the end of picturesque Mill Street, that impregnable wall, a massive man-made cliff, is even more imposing. Again, there are those who hold that the castle is best seen from across the river, looming above the quaint cottage charm of that isolated community at Bridge End, particularly colourful when autumn tints the trees.

A band of Keuper Sandstone runs north and south through central Warwickshire, and the county's three castles are on it, the northernmost of them, Maxstoke Castle, being a little gem of modern domesticity cradled in history. From it Sir John de Clinton rode out to fight at Poitiers, a building almost identical with the castle of today, save that he crossed a drawbridge where now a stone bridge spans the moat. Sir John's uncle, William de Clinton, later the Earl of Huntingdon, built the red sandstone castle around 1346.

Humphrey, the first Duke of Buckingham, gave the Clintons two Northamptonshire manors in exchange for Maxstoke. Eventually he rode out of the quadrangle with battlemented walls, beneath the three-storeyed gatehouse, and across that moat to die for the Lancastrian cause in 1460, leaving his title and castle to his grandson Henry. After helping the Yorkist, Richard III, to the throne, Duke Henry changed the white rose for the red only to be captured and executed at Salisbury while preparing the way for Henry Tudor, Earl of Richmond, in his bid to oust Richard.

Shakespeare resurrects Buckingham as one of the ghosts around

Richard's tent on the eve of Bosworth prophesying death to the king and victory for Henry Tudor:

> *God, and good angels, fight on Richmond's side,*
> *And Richard falls in height of all his pride.*

Maxstoke Castle is inextricably linked with Bosworth Field, across the county boundary in Leicestershire, and the change of dynasties it occasioned. It had become Crown property on Duke Henry's execution, and Richard III stayed there a night on his way to Nottingham before going to his death at Bosworth, while Henry Tudor, as Henry VII, slept in the octagonal room of the Ladye Tower after the battle. A chair is shown at Maxstoke in which Henry is said to have been crowned on the battlefield of Bosworth, but its authenticity is doubtful. Seven miles from Maxstoke, the Three Tuns Inn at Atherstone has a Bosworth reference on its otherwise ordinary sign because Henry Tudor is believed to have slept there on the night before the battle. It features his red Welsh dragon, the white boar of Richard III, and crossed swords with the date 1485, while behind the bar there is a painted mural of the battle.

The Maxstoke estates were restored by Henry VII to Duke Henry's son, Edward, third Duke of Buckingham, but the family misfortunes were not yet ended. His mother was Catherine Woodville, sister to Edward IV's queen, Elizabeth Woodville. This left the third duke too close to the royal line for the peace of mind of Henry VIII when he succeeded, so he charged the duke with treason and executed him in 1521. Again Maxstoke was vested in the Crown, but if any of its owners have earned the right to haunt it my vote goes to the ill-fated second duke, Henry, for haunted it is reputed to be.

Maxstoke was more a fortified dwelling house than the grim defensive castle of earlier days despite its four strong towers, Ladye Tower, Kitchen Tower, Dairy Tower, and Deadman's Tower, so called because a skeleton was found there. Built into the north-west corner of the courtyard are the living quarters with later additions to the original structure. The letters D.W.M. above the date 1698, high in this corner, stand for Dilke and William III and Mary.

Fetherston-Dilke is one of the best-known names in Warwickshire, associated with Maxstoke Castle and Packwood House, near Knowle, and it is worth a few moments' patience with a pedigree to understand how the Dilkes and Fetherstons became linked.

It was a William Dilke of Maxstoke who married a Mary Fetherston-Leigh of the Fetherston family from Packwood. In 1769 their son, Thomas, inherited Packwood under the will of his mother's unmarried half-sister, Catherine Fetherston-Leigh, and took the name of Fetherston. His niece, Frances Mary Fetherston, married her cousin, John Dilke, who also took his wife's surname, and it was their son, Charles, who, inheriting Maxstoke under the will of Captain Thomas Dilke, first took the name of Fetherston-Dilke—a precedent followed by Mr. Beaumont Percival when he inherited Maxstoke. Captain C. B. Fetherston-Dilke, R.N. now occupies the castle.

One of the treasures of Maxstoke is Amy Robsart's bed which came from Cumnor Hall, Berkshire, where that unhappy clandestine wife of Robert Dudley, Earl of Leicester, fell to her death.

Critics often ask why history is taught in schools; why dates, why names of kings and queens. To look around Maxstoke is sufficient answer. The cavalry boots worn by a Fetherston at the Battle of the Boyne; the table once belonging to Sir Everard Digby round which the Gunpowder plotters schemed; the portrait of Mary Fetherston-Leigh, great-niece of Jane Lane who accompanied Charles II on his escape from the Boscobel Oak—these things come alive to the student of history.

Maxstoke has a strange wonderfully-carved 'whispering door', actually two doors opening in an angle of a room and having a common jamb. It was salvaged from Kenilworth Castle, a dozen miles to southward, after the 'slighting', when a gaping hole was blown in the north wall of the Norman keep by the Parliamentarians to render the castle indefensible by the Royalists. There is more elaborate carving, in stone, on the fireplace of the great hall of Maxstoke. Decorated with the Dilke arms, it bears several inscriptions: 'Where no wood is, ye fire goeth out' and 'No tale bearers, strife ceaseth' seem to imply the same thing. The Latin *'Pennatus sidera morte'* translates as 'Winged to the stars by death', and is a reminder that one Fetherston at least died in the Civil War—Sir

Timothy, beheaded at Chester after the second Battle of Worcester in 1651.

Like many large homes Maxstoke Castle had its own jester, and a miniature is kept of the last of these merry fellows along with a replica of his bauble. He was Tom Grainger who died in 1681, leaving descendants at Fillongley until recent years. The castle is moat-encircled, and across the moat nowadays is a golf course. From one of the towers above the moat a Cavalier once made a spectacular escape down a rope—but it was part of a film, *The Golden Spur*, made by the BBC for Children's Hour.

There is one surpassing way to see Kenilworth Castle for the first time, by approaching it across country from Honiley as I once did with a Danish girl who had seen much of England during a prolonged stay. She was entranced as the castle came in view, honey-coloured in the sunlight, and voted it the loveliest thing she had seen in England.

Turn down the road to Honiley Church at the Boot Inn. About one hundred yards before the road turns right at the church drive there is on your left a plank across the ditch, and a stile in the hedge, but first visit the church for the pleasure of the blue-tinted east window with its peacock sign-manual of Mrs. Saintsbury from Cornwall—it appears again in Packwood and Knowle churches nearby. The footpath on the one-inch map is difficult to find, but if you aim for the well-marked track at the south-west corner of the Chase Wood you will follow hedges to the stream crossing near that spot. It is then a straightforward walk of two miles on the track south of Chase Wood, with the mellow romantic walls of Kenilworth Castle beckoning at every stride. Within half a mile of the castle, where the map shows The Pleasance, you cross a water-logged ditch, once one of the ornamental waterways surrounding this raised pleasure garden of the castle. Here Sir Walter Scott placed one of the most dramatic scenes in English literature, after Robert Dudley, Earl of Leicester, had declared his love for Queen Elizabeth I.

'No Dudley', said Elizabeth, yet it was with broken accents. 'No, I must be the mother of my people. Other ties that make the lowly maiden happy are denied to her Sovereign'.

So, sorrowfully, the Queen dismissed Leicester, but while she gazed after him a young woman threw herself at Elizabeth's feet and claimed her protection—Amy Robsart, Countess of Leicester, the bride to whom the earl was secretly married and who was so soon to die, possibly murdered at her husband's command. Scott took liberty with the facts, but he gives a fair description of the splendid celebrations when Leicester entertained his Queen at Kenilworth in July 1575, the culminating occasion in the history of a castle so soon to be largely destroyed.

The many Irishmen in the Midlands might well give the ruins of Kenilworth a long look, evidence as they are that Cromwell's vandalism was not restricted to Ireland. It was because Cromwell could not afford to maintain both his army in Ireland and his garrisons in previously-Royalist castles in England that, along with other castles, Kenilworth was 'slighted'. The wall of the Norman keep was blown out and the castle roofs stripped, thus causing Kenilworth to become the picturesque ruin it still is.

Furthermore, the Parliamentary leader, Colonel Hawksworth, wrecked the dam impounding the waters of two brooks to make the protective mere half incircling the castle on the south, which rendered Kenilworth the most impregnable of English lake castles. This draining of the lake was to provide Hawksworth with 111 more acres of pasture for his castle, and the old basin, perfectly distinguishable to the discerning eye, is still used for grazing.

Magnificent as were the Elizabethan festivities at Kenilworth, the floating islands of nymphs on the lake and 320 hogsheads of beer to cheer the multitude, the castle had its greatest period 700 years ago. Then, from the Battle of Lewes on 15 May 1264 until the Battle of Evesham on 4 August 1265, the master of Kenilworth, Simon de Montfort, was ruler of England. Simon married Eleanor, sister of Henry III who, in 1248, gave her Kenilworth Castle. As the years progressed Simon found himself in increasing opposition to his royal brother-in-law, whom he charged with autocratic misgovernment. Simon himself was anxious to set up representative government, in which he was so far successful as to be dubbed 'Father of the British Parliament'.

At Lewes, Sussex, Simon captured Henry III and his son, Edward, but the prince escaped and by August 1265 brought together the royal army for a showdown with de Montfort, who was with his forces near Evesham in Worcestershire awaiting reinforcement by his son, young Simon. The strategy of Prince Edward, later Edward I, was to engage the two de Montfort armies separately, so he moved towards Kenilworth and young Simon. Unaware of Edward's approach, young Simon camped in the meadows outside Kenilworth instead of seeking the security of the castle walls. In a surprise attack Edward routed his enemy, Simon having to evade capture by swimming the lake in his nightshirt.

Carrying the banners of the defeated army, Edward set out for Evesham where Simon de Montfort was glad to see apparently friendly forces approaching. Too late he realized the stratagem.

'Now may God have our souls, for our bodies are theirs', he said as he went into battle to die.

His son remained in possession of Kenilworth, and at midsummer, 1266, Edward besieged the castle, bringing up battering engines and barges, setting up a wooden tower with 200 bowmen, and producing the Archbishop of Canterbury to excommunicate the garrison. Not until Christmas, compelled by disease and starvation, did Simon surrender, going into exile with his two brothers while Henry III gave Kenilworth Castle to his second son, Edmund, founder of the Lancastrian branch of the House of Plantagenet.

During the Plantagenet regime Edward II was held captive at Kenilworth before being moved to Berkeley Castle in Gloucestershire and murdered. John of Gaunt, the great Lancastrian, gave Kenilworth its splendid banqueting hall—the best of its kind and period after Westminster Hall. If it seems somewhat diminished to the visitor today he must remember that the grass on which he stands is in the cellar beneath the hall, the fireplace and windows of which are a storey above. On their level the original size of the hall can be better appreciated than from below.

When John of Gaunt's son, Henry IV, assumed the throne, Kenilworth Castle again came into royal hands, and it was Henry V who cleared a marshy tract to construct The Pleasance, a place of dalliance and whispered romance. Henry VIII did some building at Kenilworth, but there is a certain rough justice in that the man who destroyed so much in England failed to leave his mark on Kenilworth. No trace of King Henry VIII's lodgings remain today.

After the stirring days of Robert Dudley and Cromwell Kenilworth's ruins reverted to the Crown again, and Charles II gave what

21 *John of Gaunt's Hall, Kenilworth Castle, built by Robert Skyllington in the fourteenth century*

was left to the Hyde family of his chief minister, Lord Clarendon. There was a curious episode in the eighteenth century when ribbon workers and weavers from Coventry squatted in the castle and set up their looms, evidence of which can be seen in holes in the walls of Leicester's Building. They were the last inhabitants of the castle except for various occupants of Leicester's Gatehouse. In 1937 Sir John Siddeley, later Lord Kenilworth, bought the castle from the 6th Earl of Clarendon and gave it to the nation.

Today's vandalism is tomorrow's history. If I see someone scratching his name in the sandstone walls of Kenilworth Castle that is vandalism, and I remonstrate. If I read on those same walls names inscribed a century ago, out comes my notebook and I record J. Edkins, saddler, 1789; T. Stratford, painter; and W. and C. Pratt, collar-makers, who carved their names on the winding steps off the Great Hall in 1813. Can one look with other than sympathy on 'Sophie and Papa, December 1854' or on three names neatly bracketed in 1865, 'J. Draper, H. Robbins, A Cordery—ad amicitiam, H.R.fecit'?

The imaginative can easily people Kenilworth's bare shell with ghosts of long ago. At high noon there is the colour and shouting of the tournament as jousting knights clash on the dam beneath Mortimer's Tower, and as owls hoot in the trees and bats flit among the jagged walls the sensitive ear can still pick up the silken rustle of a Tudor maiden bound for a tryst in The Pleasance.

Scott is said to have begun his novel *Kenilworth* at the 'King's Arms and Castle' in the town, and his bedroom retains the furniture and a four-poster of the period. The intriguing 'Virgins and Castle' marked the lodging of Queen Elizabeth's maidens when she stayed at Kenilworth Castle, but one pub name in the town has nothing to do with local history. This is the Wyandotte Inn, built by John Boddington, whose son had emigrated to America and, by 1867, settled in Wyandotte, Michigan. So the father named his inn after his son's home, the name also of a breed of fowl and an Indian tribe.

Kenilworth has a lesser-known ruin than its castle, the Augustinian establishment in the Abbey Fields, dissolved by Henry VIII. Today its ruins incorporate one of the few collapsing clapper stiles in the county.

22 *St. Mary's Tower, and Castle Street, with an inn sign*
   reminder of Warwick's horse-racing associations

If you have left a car at Honiley there is a pleasant walk of three miles by field paths from Kenilworth to Beausale which will test your eye for country, followed by a couple of miles by lanes, completing a round walk of eight miles.

Three miles along the Warwick road from Kenilworth stands the Saxon Mill Restaurant, a place to compare with Rupert Brooke's 'Grantchester', where the Avon froths round a mill wheel and foams down a weir with

> '... the thrilling-sweet and rotten
> Unforgettable, unforgotten
> River smell.'

Opposite the Saxon Mill across the road rises a knoll known as Blacklow Hill, surmounted by a memorial erected in 1821 by the local squire, Bertie Greathead. Elders grow in the hollow at its base, snowdrops cluster there in February, followed soon by the cuckoo pint or 'lords and ladies'.

There were several lords but no ladies in that sinister hollow on 20 June 1312, for despite a plaque which declares 1 July the date when Blacklow Hill found its blood-stained niche in history, historians are unanimously in favour of the earlier date. The Earls of Lancaster, Arundel, and Hereford were certainly there, all young, and among them another young man in his 29th year, a tall, strong figure, though his handsome, foreign face showed signs of dissipation and ravages of fear. He was Piers Gaveston, a Gascon, favourite of Edward II. Received at the Court of Edward I, he was the constant companion of the Prince of Wales, and together they plumbed such depths of profligacy that the king banished Gaveston from Britain. The first act of Edward II was to recall his friend and create him Earl of Cornwall. Other honours piled on him, earning him the hatred of a group of powerful earls who forced the king to send Gaveston into exile, which Edward did by creating him his Lieutenant in Ireland.

By 1312 a state approaching civil war existed and the earls captured Gaveston at Scarborough. Taking him to London, they stopped one night at Deddington rectory in Oxfordshire, and there Guy Beauchamp, Earl of Warwick, broke in and greeted Gaveston with the sinister threat: 'The Black Dog of Arden is come to keep his oath that you should one day feel his teeth'. Gaveston had been in the habit of referring to Warwick as the 'Black Dog of Arden'. Now, in a dungeon at Warwick Castle, he waited while his enemies deliberated on his fate. Eventually he was led to Blacklow Hill where his head was struck off and taken to Kenilworth Castle while the body was carried back to Warwick on a ladder.

St. Mary's soaring tower gives Warwick the dignity of a cathedral city, while Caesar's Tower and Guy's Tower, rising from the trees of the castle grounds, invest it with the strength of a fortress. Ethelfleda, daughter of King Alfred, the 'Lady of the Mercians', founded Warwick in 914, and her mound can still be seen at the west end of the castle grounds, originally a ditched and palisaded frontier fortress against the Danes. Only two years after the Conquest William the Conqueror constructed a motte and bailey which, during the next two centuries saw some additional stone building. This is not a prominent feature, however, and the castle is seen, as a spectacular fortification of the fourteenth and fifteenth centuries, with lofty towers in the angles, enclosing an attractive Jacobean residence surrounded by the indigenous trees of leafy Warwickshire, with exotic introductions.

William Rufus created Henry de Newburgh the first Earl of Warwick, and his great grandson, the second Henry de Newburgh was one of the barons who supported the much-maligned King John. After four generations the male line of the Newburghs died out, and the castle and title went, for one disastrous earldom, to William Mauduit, who backed the wrong side during Simon de Montfort's ascendancy over Henry III, watched Warwick Castle destroyed by the enemy from Kenilworth, and paid heavily in cash for his release from captivity.

His nephew, a Worcestershire Beauchamp, succeeded, first of a line of six earls, all great powers in the land. Their banner of six golden crosslets and bar on a red field flew over major reconstruction work at the castle, including the great towers. Guy Beauchamp, the 'Black Dog of Arden', gave his name to Guy's Tower, built earlier along with Caesar's Tower by two Thomas Beauchamps, dealt with more fully along with the illustrious Richard Beauchamp when we visit St. Mary's Church. The last Beauchamp, Henry, had he lived, might have proved the 'Kingmaker' that his brother-in-law, Richard Neville, became. Henry VI created him Duke of Warwick and King of the Isle of Wight, titles which lapsed on his untimely death at 22.

The earldom of Warwick went through Anne Beauchamp to the Nevilles in the formidable person of her husband Richard, who was better known by his wife's title of Warwick than his paternal title of Salisbury, and, of course, best known as the 'Kingmaker'. After his death on the battlefield of Barnet in 1471, Warwick Castle passed to 'false fleeting perjured Clarence', who gave it a tower named after him, and to Richard of Gloucester, who built in part the Bear Tower.

After a period of skulduggery typical of his reign, Henry VIII created John Dudley Earl of Warwick—of whom the less said the better. The green lion device of the Dudleys endured through his more worthy son, Ambrose, at whose death without issue, despite three marriages, the earldom again disappeared. Following a lapse of 16 years the castle was bestowed by James I on Sir Fulke Greville, the wealthy M.P. for Warwickshire, with the title Baron Brooke of Beauchamp Court. He gave the castle its Jacobean domesticity. Castle and earldom were divorced, the Rich family being Earls of Warwick until 1759 when, on the death of the last Rich, the eighth Baron Brooke, another Fulke Greville, was granted the earldom, so that castle and title were reunited, and have remained so in the Brooke family up to the present and seventh Earl.

In the earlier years of this century Warwick Castle gave one of its most intriguing figures to the county and the nation in the comely person of Frances, the fifth Earl's countess. Close friend of Edward VII, a gay leader of society in both drawing-room and hunting field, she suddenly announced her conversion to socialism. Her sincerity led to her foregoing hunting and banning it on her estates, to her giving up wearing furs and feathers and becoming a vegetarian, and to her selling her jewellery to help finance Labour parliamentary candidates. In 1923 she fought Warwick for Labour, polling only 4,000 votes against 16,000 for the winning Conservative, Anthony Eden. She died aged 77 in 1938, a disappointed woman because her plan to convert her Essex home, Easton Lodge, into a Labour college had never matured for lack of funds.

Warwick's medieval splendour still overcomes its modern traffic at West Gate where the pavement drops darkly through solid rock beneath the twelfth-century chapel of Leicester's Hospital, which raises its gabled black and white timbers above a tall railed wall. It was once written of Robert Dudley that he was 'without courage, without talent, and without virtue'. He was, however, well endowed with cunning. Having acquired from the townsfolk of Warwick the group of buildings at West Gate previously held by the guilds, he convinced Queen Elizabeth that it would stimulate recruiting if she provided a place where her old soldiers could live their declining years in comfort. So in 1571 she granted a charter for the founding of the Lord Leicester Hospital, leaving her favourite to draw up his own regulations for its conduct. Dudley thereupon laid it down that the 12 'brethren' of the hospital should be selected from Warwick, Kenilworth, Stratford, and certain parishes in south Gloucestershire—all his own properties, so that the recruiting impetus was into his private army of retainers.

Today, retired men are taken from all three services, living in their own quarters free of charge and with a heating allowance. Married couples are admitted, but no children. Uniform is supplied, an Elizabethan-style hat, cloak, and a scarf with a silver badge of the Warwickshire bear. Applicants must be service pensioners, disabled or aged, but mobile because the brethren act as guides to visitors.

Since 1958 great restoration has been undertaken at the hospital, most important being the renovation of the Great Hall and its opening for functions, thus restoring it to the public purposes to which it was put centuries ago.

The earliest of the Leicester Hospital buildings is the chapel over West Gate with a stall for each of the brethren. Built in 1123, it became the chapel of the Guild of St. George, to which in 1383 the guilds of the Holy Trinity and the Virgin Mary were joined to form the United Guilds of Warwick. Around 1309 the United Guilds built the Great Hall and the Guild Hall, and it was the latter which Dudley partitioned to accommodate his first dozen brethren. Henry VIII disbanded the guilds in 1546, but the Master of the United Guilds of Warwick saved their property from the Crown by making it over to the burgesses of Warwick who, not sure what to do with the Great Hall, allowed King's School to function in it. Since then it has been put to menial usage, but now, restored to its former glories it will bestow dignity on any function. Off the Minstrels Gallery a smaller room, available for more intimate parties, commands fine views stretching from the winning post on Warwick racecourse to the distant Cotswolds. The Guild Hall stands much as it did 600 years ago. Along one wall is a semi-circle of swords left by deceased brethren, including two which belonged to the guards of the last King of Poland in the eighteenth century.

The hereditary patron of the hospital is Viscount de L'Isle, head of the Sidney family, whose porcupine crest adorns the courtyard wall. To enter this galleried courtyard is to step back down the four centuries that the Lord Leicester Hospital has thrown open its doors in hospitality—the original non-medical meaning of 'hospital'. Around its wall in ancient lettering are the injunctions, 'Honour all Men'; 'Love the Brotherhood'; 'Fear God'; and 'Honour the King', and above the door, 'Be kindly affectioned one toward another'.

Warwick runs busily from West Gate, along High Street and Jury Street, to East Gate, also surmounted by a chapel, St. Peter's. This is now part of Warwick High School for Girls, whose buildings span 700 years. The rugged base of East Gate is fifteenth century, its chapel being built in the reign of Henry VI; two half-timbered cottages used as cloak rooms and music rooms are Elizabethan; the headmistress's study is in gracious Queen Anne 'Landor House', birthplace of the poet, Walter Savage Landor; and the school also has the modern laboratories, gymnasium, and other buildings one would expect at so progressive an establishment.

Across St. Nicholas Meadows and beyond the river, Warwick School also has associations with a poet, John Masefield being among the illustrious Old Warwickians. A public school for boys, Warwick School confronts the visitor with a statue of Edward the Confessor, a reminder that it is the only school in England with documentary evidence of continuous existence since before the Norman Conquest. During autumn term the school has a picturesque annual ceremony when the town crier of Warwick pays his visit to plead for the Mayor's half holiday. Wearing his tricorn hat he calls the entire school around him in the Quad, and reads the traditional request for the holiday. This done, he goes to the Headmaster's study and returns with him to the Quad with the good news that the holiday is granted. Finally he visits each formroom, where the boys show their gratitude by dropping largesse into the tricorn hat.

Granting the school coat of arms, the College of Heralds accepted A.D. 914 as the school's foundation—the year when Ethelfleda built the Burgh of Warwick.

For all Warwick's attractions it is St. Mary's tower, rising above its roofs, which dominates the town, giving grace and distinction to so many views around, particularly that which bursts on the traveller from Birmingham at the top of Hatton Hill. The earlier tower and nave of St. Mary's were destroyed in 1694 in the fire which claimed over 200 Warwick houses. The rebuilding of the nave was completed in 1704, and the present tower, built on arches over the street, was designed by Sir Christopher Wren for a £10 fee. Born in Warwick, I had my infant image of a church formed by St. Mary's—essentially an image of a museum of mouldering battle flags. Those I knew, the colours of volunteers raised to repel Napoleonic invasion, and the rustling ghosts of standards transparent with age in the Royal Warwickshire Regiment's chapel, have been augmented by recent additions. A huge off-white ensign now hangs in the south-west corner of St. Mary's above the shelves from which the loaves of the Bissett, Smith, and Johnson charities were distributed for 202 years to 32 old people. This ensign streamed in the face of the enemy in 60 First World War engagements, part of it being shot away at Jutland. Also at the west end is the smaller laid-up standard of the 605 (County of Warwick) Squadron, whose Vampires screamed about Midland skies earlier in the Jet Age.

We have to thank the Hundred Years War for St. Mary's. To it went Thomas Beauchamp, Earl of Warwick, to distinguish himself on a beach-head at La Hogue when he led a party of eight to rout a French strongpoint held by 100, thus enabling 30,000 invading English to go ashore unhindered. Thomas was in the front line at Crecy with the Black Prince, and at Poitiers he took a number of prisoners, with whose ransom money he began rebuilding Warwick's ancient collegiate chapel, so it is apt that St. Mary's, where a spacious light nave looks to a narrow gloomy chancel, has become a soldiers' church. The founder himself, dying at Calais, was brought back to rest in the chancel.

His son, another Thomas, continued the building of St. Mary's choir, but his lasting fame is to be found in the muzzle worn by the bear which, with its baculus or ragged staff, is Warwickshire's emblem. This younger Thomas had been the guardian of Richard II, but quarrelling with the king, he was imprisoned in the Tower of London, where Beauchamp's Tower takes its name from the place of his captivity. One day during the quarrel the enraged king swore 'I cannot muzzle you, but I will muzzle your bear.' So it is the muzzled bear, alongside a brass to young Thomas, which in St. Mary's decorates the portal of that masterpiece of medieval ecclesiastical art, the Beauchamp Chapel.

The central monument in the chapel is to the son of the younger Thomas, Richard Beauchamp, Earl of Warwick, who lies in effigy, his head resting on his helmet with a swan crest. This he bore in many jousts, but he dispensed with it near Calais when, on two consecutive days, he entered the lists in disguise and defeated noted champions, completing the hat-trick on the third day in his own armour. He sent a war horse and a large sum of money to each knight he had beaten. Richard served in Henry v's wars in France. He missed Agincourt by one day while conducting prisoners to England, and was Governor of Rouen when Joan of Arc went to the stake there. On 30 April 1439 Richard, too, died at Rouen, and was brought home with great ceremony for burial at Warwick in the chapel he was building.

It is said that after 200 years the floor of the Beauchamp Chapel collapsed, to reveal Richard's body unsullied by time—but only for a moment. Then it crumbled to dust, though a tale is told that there were women in Warwick who made themselves rings of Richard's hair, pilfered from the cave-in.

The tomb and its surroundings are now quite resplendent, with Richard astonishingly lifelike, for among those who helped build his memorial was Roger Webb of the Worshipful Company of Barber-Surgeons. Consulted on anatomy, he is responsible for the faithful representation of the veins in Richard's face and hands.

Richard Beauchamp's near neighbour in the chapel is the much less worthy Leicester, Elizabeth's favourite. After the death of his first wife, Amy Robsart, and the failure of his suit with the queen, Leicester took as his second wife Lady Douglas Sheffield—and deserted her. His third wife, Lettice, widow of the first Earl of Essex, now lies beside Leicester in the eternal amity of death. She married yet again, saw her third husband and her son, Robert of Essex, beheaded, and reached the age of 95 when she died in 1634 'upon Christmas Day in the morning'. Her epitaph in the Beauchamp Chapel records:

> *And because she tooke delight*
> *Christ's poore members to invite,*
> *He fully now requites her love*
> *And sends his angels from above;*
> *That did to Heaven her soule convay*
> *To solemnize his own birthday.*

There is also in the Beauchamp Chapel a Doom painting, fine medieval glass, a window tracery of angels carrying scrolls of music, and the miniature fan tracery of the exquisite 'Little Chantry'. Here, too, is a rarity, a wooden piscina.

Away across St. Mary's chancel the old chapter house is now filled with an elaborate memorial to Fulke Greville (1554-1628), servant to Queen Elizabeth, counsellor to James I, and friend to Sir Philip Sidney, that paragon of chivalry. Warwick also lays claim to the bones of the ancestors of Keith Holyoake, recently Prime Minister of New Zealand, whose great grandfather, Richard Holyoake, sailed with the original British settlers in 1842. The Holyoake monument, against the north aisle of St. Mary's, has a Latin inscription which translates: 'Not far from hence lie ... the Root, Shoot, and Branches of the Holy Oake, namely Francis Holyoake the Root; Thomas the only Shoot; and the Branches of Thomas and Anne, his wife, 12 in number....'

We will end our exploration of St. Mary's in the regimental chapel beneath the glowing Camm window with its ranks of troops in the uniforms of 150 years ago. The chapel speaks of the far-off lands to which the regiment has spread the renown of the county.

Among the non-military memorials at St. Mary's is a brass of Thomas Oken, a poor Warwick boy of Tudor days who became a rich mercer and a benefactor of his native town. In 1955 Oken's House in Castle Street, sixteenth century and timber-framed, with an overhang and gable, was opened as the Warwick Doll Museum with 1,000 antique dolls.

The great Norman family of the Clintons having entered this chapter with Maxstoke Castle, let us take the Birmingham road from Warwick to visit another place connected with them. In eight miles, at Chadwick End, a left turn brings us to Baddesley Clinton Church in a secluded countryside where it is difficult to believe that Birmingham is so near as the grey tower rises lonely above the trees, battlemented, buttressed, and girdled with fearsome gargoyles. Beyond the churchyard a footpath through a woodland belt leads the visitor in one of the county's most idyllic short walks to Baddesley Clinton Hall, where luck may display one of the resident peacocks spreading his breathtaking fan of tail feathers.

Pevsner writes of Baddesley Clinton Hall as 'the perfect late medieval manor house'. 'The entrance side of grey stone', he continues, 'the small creeper-clad Queen Anne brick bridge across the moat, the gateway with a porch, higher than the roof and embattled —it could not be better.' The manor of Baddesley Clinton came to the Clintons of Coleshill in 1250, and during the next century they rebuilt the original building as a semi-fortified manor house. For about one hundred years from 1438 the Bromes were in possession, and they gave Baddesley Clinton its most colourful episode.

As you enter Baddesley Clinton Church you step on Nicholas Brome's gravestone, beneath a mat, for he requested in his will that 'my body be buried within the parish church of Baddesley Clinton, where as people may tread upon mee when they come into the church.' For Brome died, in October 1517, a repentant double murderer.

He performed other acts of penitence in his lifetime. One is recorded inside the base of the church tower: 'Nicholas Brome Esq., Lord of Baddesley, did new builde this steeple in the raigne of King Henry the Seaventh'; and at Packwood Church, three miles away, he installed three bells and possibly built the tower.

The Bromes were originally tanners at Bridge End, Warwick, but John Brome, father of Nicholas, had become a worthy country gentleman and Lord of Baddesley Clinton. He was stabbed to death in London by John Herthill, steward to the Earl of Warwick, in a dispute over property. Nicholas succeeded to Baddesley Clinton, and three years later he waylaid his father's murderer at Longbridge, near Barford, and killed him. This he made amends for by paying £5 for masses at St. Mary's, Warwick, and £1 13s. 4d. to Herthill's widow. But Nicholas was a hasty-tempered man, and when, returning one day from hunting, he found the priest of Baddesley Clinton 'chucking his wife under the chin' he slew him. Hence the further acts of repentance.

Double murderer or no, Nicholas Brome appears in the fine east window at Baddesley Clinton, piously kneeling with his daughter, Constance, and her husband, Sir Edward Ferrers. This Sir Edward, who died in 1535, is the first of 12 generations of Ferrers at Baddesley Clinton commemorated in the chancel floor. The last, another Edward, died in 1890. Among the heraldic devices of the Ferrers in the east window is a shield with 32 quarterings.

Approaching from the church a right of way crosses the manor drive, goes through a gate and across the fields to the canal bridge at Kingswood Brook. A right turn into Kingswood, on to the Stratford Canal towpath behind the Boot Inn, up the locks, and a lane at the lock-keeper's cottage takes you to the road for Packwood House, a National Trust property, and beyond, by a field path, to Packwood Church where the treble bell commemorates Dr. Thomas Savage, killed in the Kingston, Jamaica, earthquake on 14 January 1907.

To Packwood Church in June 1706 came a bridal couple rather advanced in years. The bride was Sarah Ford, the bridegroom a large, robust man, a Lichfield bookseller. In the fourth year of their marriage the first son was born, to become famous as Dr. Samuel Johnson.

Packwood House qualifies for this chapter from its associations with the Fetherston family of Maxstoke. It is most renowned for its clipped yews, representing Christ preaching to the Multitude in the Sermon on the Mount. The visitor cannot but feel awe as he passes, dwarfed, between the massive forms of the Multitude towards the Master. Leaving the Apostles, he reaches a red brick path which corkscrews to its apex in a secluded nook, surrounded by yew hedges, where a seat leans against the topmost yew, known as the Master. The head gardener told me that the yews are cut, according to the weather, in ten to 20 days in August by a team of seven.

Packwood House is a sciagrapher's paradise—a sciagrapher is 'one who makes instruments for measuring time by the heavenly bodies.' Three of Packwood's sundials, always immaculately painted, are as familiar as the yews. They were established, as were the trees, around 1660 by John Fetherston on walls probably raised about 100 years earlier by his grandfather, William Fetherston, who built the bulk of the existing house. One sundial is on the wall above the forecourt. Round the corner, above the road, another facing north-east is marked with the hours four to ten and bears the motto '*Orimur; Morimur*' (We rise up; we die.). The stable sundial is marked one to eight and its motto '*Septem sine horis*' (Seven without the hours) is a reminder that the shortest night in the Midlands is barely seven hours long; seven hours during which the sun cannot cast the shadow of the gnomon on the dial.

So, where more appropriate than Packwood House to investigate a romance which has time as its theme? Packwood has its Queen Mary's Room, used by George v's consort as a retiring room when she took tea there in 1927; its Queen Margaret's Room, with a bedstead on which the Lancastrian Queen slept at Owlpen Manor, Gloucestershire, several nights before the Battle of Tewkesbury; and a General Ireton's Room, with a four-poster in which the Cromwellian general is said to have slept in that room before the Battle of Edgehill—though he was certainly not a general then.

The windows of his room give on to a vista down the one-time main drive to Packwood House, now a grass-grown avenue. There is little natural cover, so it was not surprising that a young man skulking there during Ireton's visit was seen from the bedroom window by his young son. The prowler was a youth of Cavalier sympathies in love with the daughter of the stern Parliamentarian. She, too, loved him, but young Ireton, without any consideration for his sister, raised the alarm. The imprudent lover was captured, taken to Kenilworth Castle, and condemned to be shot at curfew one night.

On the fatal evening, the general's daughter, heartbroken and desperate, climbed the steps in the belfry at Kenilworth Church and, at curfew hour, clung to the clapper of the bell to prevent its ringing, thus saving her lover. This story is told in Packwood House guidebook, described as a legend. But even a legend should be credible. Does this one bear investigation?

We are nearly all familiar with the line 'Curfew must not ring tonight'. It comes from a narrative poem by an American schoolgirl Rose Hartwick (Thorpe later by marriage). She was born in 1850, eight years after a certain Albert Smith had embodied a similar story in a play called *Blanche Heriot*. This play told a story associated with Chertsey, Surrey, during the Wars of the Roses 200 years before the Great Civil War. Rose Hartwick places the story in Cromwellian times, but without any special locality.

Why are legends perpetuated which an elementary study of history would dispel? At the time of Edgehill Ireton was only 31 years old, captain of a troop, and unlikely to have children of a romantic age. He ultimately had one son and three daughters, but from his marriage on 15 June 1646, nearly four years after Edgehill, with Cromwell's daughter, Bridget. Nor was Kenilworth Castle in Cromwellian hands in 1642.

So, if curfew does ring it tolls the death knell of the Packwood legend. What matter, so long as Packwood House still stands with its yews, its sundials, gazebos, and bee boles? It is a beautiful house, open to the public, and maybe it has its love story, though with a less happy ending than the reprieve of the young Cavalier. As we looked out on a wintry countryside from General Ireton's window the caretaker pointed out a spreading beech tree beyond the lawns.

'They say', he told me, 'that one of the Fetherston daughters, years ago, had been ill and, from her window, she saw her fiancé approaching up the drive. Rushing out to meet him, she collapsed in his arms and died beneath that tree.'

CHAPTER EIGHT

Arden

In a broad division of Warwickshire the Feldon was the section south of Stratford and the Avon, a landscape of larger fields, while Arden was the more wooded countryside north of the river. The Rev. William Gresley, born at Kenilworth in 1801, set the main events of a little-known novel, *The Forest of Arden*, as far north as Merevale Abbey, near Atherstone, and there is certainly no more imposing assembly of the authentic oaks of Arden than those studding the steep hillside above the abbey ruins, crowned by one of the county's most imposing residences, Merevale Hall. The home of the Dugdales, descended from Warwickshire's famous sixteenth-century historian, Sir William Dugdale, the hall on its lofty pinnacle is reminiscent of Belvoir Castle. It was built in the nineteenth century around the remains of a William and Mary mansion.

One of the rivers of Arden, the Blythe, flows placidly to its confluence with the Cole at Prosser's Mill, skirting on its last mile Blyth Hall, home long ago of the historian, and now of Sir William Dugdale, the 2nd Baronet, who succeeded his father in 1965, but did not move to Merevale. The two seats are some seven miles apart by a road which has at least two particular associations with the Dugdales. At Bentley, the sign of the Horse and Jockey Inn shows the present Sir William riding Cloncarrig in the 1952 Grand National. Close to the inn a ruined wall of Holy Trinity Chapel rises in a field at Chapel Farm, and nearby are boundary stones, one dated 1866, the other bearing the initials W.F.S.D., grandfather of the present baronet. He was William Stratford Dugdale, and he has left a more glorious memorial than this stone half hidden in a hedge. At Baxterley Church, two miles northward, a shining brass commemorates two men entombed by fire in Baxterley Pit on 1 May 1882, and nine others who perished attempting to rescue them—

the leader of these brave men being William Stratford Dugdale.

Merevale Abbey has fallen into ruin since its surrender by Abbot William to Henry VIII's commissioners, and Abbey Farm occupies the site of the old monastic buildings, even incorporating some of the ruined walls. The best preserved part of the abbey is the roofless refectory, though two pear trees rise from the thick grass within its jagged walls, where steps still remain to the platform from which a lector read aloud during meals. At the foot of a lawn is one of the monks' fishponds, bright with yellow brandy-bottle lilies. Merevale's extant church, approached through an archway, was originally the gate chapel of the abbey and had a much-venerated image of the Virgin to which such crowds flocked to pray for protection from the Black Death that people nearly died in the crush.

Merevale Abbey was founded in 1184 by Robert, Earl Ferrers. A fine brass representing one of his kinsmen, also a Robert, with his wife Margaret, lies in the chancel of the church, one of six 'gravestones with brass' known to have been in the abbey at the Dissolution. The effigy of another Earl Ferrers, William, who died in 1254, was also removed, but not until 1850 did the missing part of the right leg, now restored, turn up among the ruins. That Merevale's troubles did not end with the Dissolution is exemplified in the fourteenth-century Jesse glass of the east window, which had to be hidden from the Cromwellian depredators in the Parliamentary Wars. It was dug up from the grounds of Merevale Hall when the danger had passed.

The earlier Sir William Dugdale—the historian—was born in 1605 at Shustoke, near Blyth Hall, which he bought soon after his marriage at the age of 18. He became friendly with the Leicestershire topographer, William Burton, and with Sir Simon Archer who pressed Dugdale into helping collect material for a history of Warwickshire which he had undertaken to write. Visiting London with Archer, Dugdale found entrée to Court circles and held various appointments under Charles I, whom he accompanied to Oxford when it became the Royalist headquarters. With his estate sequestrated by the Parliamentarians and his pension from the king unpaid, he subsisted on his fees as a heraldic undertaker, arranging sumptuous funerals for persons of quality. He also studied painstakingly in various Oxford libraries, and produced other monumental works before his *Antiquities of Warwickshire* in 1656. Because of his skill in making use of the writings of others one critic dubbed Dugdale 'that grand plagiary'.

At the Restoration Dugdale proclaimed Charles II king at Coleshill on 10 May 1660, and was appointed Norroy King-of-Arms. Anticipating Burke and Debrett, Dugdale published an important genealogical work, *The Baronye of England* in 1675-6. In 1677 he was created Garter King-of-Arms and knighted, continuing his writings on history and heraldry up to his death, which overtook him seated on his chair at Blyth Hall on 10 February 1686, and was brought on by his 'tarrying too long in the meadows near his house.'

From his meadows Sir William would have seen Coleshill's spire on its hill a mile to the south-west, a spire 15 feet shorter than it was before lightning damage in 1550. It was ultimately rebuilt in 1888, 170 feet tall, to become the finest in Warwickshire after St. Michael's, Coventry.

Coleshill is long and narrow, built on either side of the steeply-sloping road from Coventry to Lichfield, and the vista downhill is filled, not unpleasantly, by the huge bobbins of Hams Hall Power Station. A by-pass has taken much of the traffic from this main street. A pillory and whipping post survives in Church Hill, where some new building development beside the church is perhaps the worst item of philistinism in the county, destroying completely the grace and character of the area.

Domesday Book describes Coleshill as a 'royal demesne', and this passed from Henry II in 1155 to Osbert de Clinton—of the family whose name occurs throughout Arden. With Joan de Clinton the Manor of Coleshill passed by marriage to the de Montforts, who held it until Sir Simon de Montfort was hanged at Tyburn for supporting the claim of Perkin Warbeck to the throne of Henry VII. One Simon Digby, in his capacity as Deputy Constable of the Tower of London, had the good luck to be de Montfort's gaoler, for to him the king made over the Coleshill estate. Digby was something of a turncoat, for he supported the Yorkists under Edward IV, but when Henry Tudor, Earl of Richmond, appeared he changed sides dramatically and, with his six brothers, fought for the Lancastrians at Bosworth in 1485.

Simon's great great grandson, Sir Robert Digby, was fortunate in

23   *Leycester's Hospital, Warwick, with St. James's Chapel perched above West Gate*

leaving the Gunpowder plotters in time to avoid the fate which overtook his kinsman, Sir Everard Digby, and James I created Robert's son Lord Digby of Geashill in King's County, Ireland, in 1618. His brother John, despite the failure of his embassy to Spain to arrange a marriage between the Infanta and Prince Charles, later Charles I, was created Lord Digby of Sherborne, Dorset, and later Earl of Bristol, honours which ended with his grandson, though there was a later creation of the barony in 1765 when Henry, the 7th Lord Digby of Geashill, because also Lord Digby of Sherborne, and Viscount Coleshill and Earl Digby of Lincoln. The viscountcy and the earldom soon died, but the present head of the family is the 12th Baron Digby of Geashill and Baron Digby of Sherborne.

The genealogist can enjoy himself among the Digby tombs in the beautiful pellucid light of the Perpendicular windows in Coleshill chancel. More simply, I found a link with the Coleshill Digbys while cruising on the Grand Canal in Ireland, where a Digby Bridge near Osberstown, County Kildare, is a reminder that Sir Robert, the prudent Gunpowder plotter, became M.P. for Athy in that same county in 1613, that his wife inherited the Irish title, Baroness Offaly, that Digbys clustered thick on the lush pastures of the east Midlands of Ireland, and, specifically, that the Rev. Benjamin Digby of Osberstown married an heiress there.

The Norman font in Coleshill Church is described as the finest in the county, but the church's abiding claim to affectionate regard is the way in which it seems to attract the roofs of Coleshill to gather companionably beneath its spire as one looks uphill from the medieval bridge of six arches at the bottom of the High Street.

Before quitting Coleshill let us take a backward look down the main street at Hams Hall Power Station, named after a mansion that stands 70 miles away near Cirencester in Gloucestershire. Sir Charles Adderley, an equerry to Charles I, bought the original Hams Hall, Lea Marston, about three miles due north of Coleshill. In 1760 the reigning Adderley completed the building of a new large residence for which he retained the name of Hams Hall. In this home Charles Bowyer Adderley, later the 1st Lord Norton, prepared a constitution for New Zealand while he was Under Secretary for the Colonies in 1866-68. This became known as the Hams Draft.

Standing empty after the First World War, Hams Hall was brought to the notice of Oswald Harrison, a shipping magnate, who had been seeking a residence in the Vale of White Horse country in Gloucestershire from which he could ride with Earl Bathurst's hounds. Failing to find such a home, he bought Hams Hall, demolished it, and moved it lock, stock and barrel to the village of Coates near Cirencester, where it was faithfully reconstructed. Today Hams Hall is a hall of residence for students of the Royal Agricultural College, Cirencester, retaining its New Zealand associations in its new name, Bledisloe Lodge, after Viscount Bledisloe of Lydney, one-time Governor-General of New Zealand, who later became a governor of the Royal Agricultural College.

Hams Hall, when it stood at Lea Marston, was half encircled by the Tame, a river, shared with Staffordshire, in which Warwickshire can take little pride. It has the unenviable reputation of being, perhaps, the most polluted river in Britain. North of Lea Marston the Tame oozes beneath the bluff on which stands the village of Kingsbury, once graced by a castle of the Kings of Mercia. Kingsbury Mill was rated at 9s. 3d. in Domesday Book, and in Henry II's reign Amabel Fitzwalter gave it 'with her body for sepulture' to the nuns of Polesworth. In more recent centuries Kingsbury Mill has been a gun-barrel mill in Napoleonic times, a saw mill, paper mill, leather mill, and finally an electrified grain mill. Beside it, Hemlingford Bridge, bearing the name of one of the old hundreds of Warwickshire, has on its cutwaters the names of subscribers who built it in 1783. The fields of the Tame valley hereabouts produce large crops of potatoes, but there are also large tracts of tortured earth with vast pits supplying sand and gravel for civil engineering projects. Fortunately the Central Electricity Generating Board is only too pleased to fill in these holes eventually with ash from Hams Hall Power Station.

Between Coleshill and Maxstoke Castle the adventurous walker can find the overgrown track of the Whitacre and Hampton-in-Arden Railway, the Stonebridge Branch that was, and follow it, unofficially, as through a jungle up the Blythe valley. An unobtrusive pastoral line, its birth and early years were fiercely contentious, for it was the first competitive railway in the British Isles. In the 1830s the London and Birmingham Railway was operating with such success that other lines wanted to run their trains on it to London. The Midland Counties Railway was making provision for this by constructing a line from Leicester to join the London and Birmingham at Rugby, while the North Midland Railway proposed doing this by a track from Derby through Tamworth to Whitacre, with a Stonebridge Branch to continue from Whitacre to a junction with the London and Birmingham at Hampton-in-Arden. This Derby-Hampton line opened to traffic on 12 August 1839, while the Midland Counties Leicester-Rugby route came into operation on 1 July 1840, competition becoming so furious that a second-class passenger was charged only 1s. and a first-class passenger 2s. over the Derby-Hampton section instead of the proper local fares of 6s. and 8s. The conflict was a major reason for the incorporation on 10 May 1844 of the North Midland, the Midland Counties, and the Birmingham and Derby Junction lines into the Midland Railway.

Another abandoned railway track in Arden, so remote that it intrigues more walkers than motorists, is the four miles of the Henley-in-Arden Branch. Leaving the main Birmingham-Paddington line at Rowington, south of Lapworth Station (called Kingswood until changed to avoid confusion with another Kingswood Station in Gloucestershire), the branch was started privately in 1861 but abandoned after five years for lack of funds. More than 30 years later the Great Western Railway completed it and opened it on 6 June 1894. The journey from Lapworth to Henley Old Station took only 13 minutes for there were no intervening stations. Talk of one at Lowsonford was stopped by the First World War—and so was the railway. The metals were lifted for use behind the trenches in France, but the ship carrying them across the Channel was sunk. In 1900 the North Warwickshire line under threat in late 1971— was opened from Tyseley to Bearley. Henley's present station was built on it and the old station sidetracked by continuing the Henley Branch across the Stratford Road by the bridge demolished in the 1960s.

Normally uneventful, the branch provided a minor news item when a 14-coach train proved too heavy for the stop block at Henley and the engine, driven by 'Hoppy' Rogers, nearly fell in the River Alne.

Yet another abandoned railway hereabouts is the Alcester Railway, opened in 1876 from a junction with the North Warwickshire at Bearley to connect Stratford-upon-Avon with Alcester. A close companion of the River Alne, it ran through Aston Cantlow, Great Alne, and Kinwarton. Its maintenance was handed to the Great Western in the year after its opening, but time took its toll and the track has long been surrendered to the brambles and the bullfinches.

Back near the River Blythe four miles south of Coleshill stands Packington Hall, home of one of the Midland noblemen best known to the public—Charles Ian Finch-Knightley, 11th Earl of Aylesford. County Commissioner for Warwickshire Boy Scouts he is a familiar figure on Scouting occasions wearing the kilt of the Black Watch, with which regiment he was wounded in Sicily. Lord Warden of the Woodmen of Arden, founded by the 3rd Earl in 1785, he is often seen with his longbow at the woodmen's headquarters, the Forest Hall, where his estate, Packington Park, brings a tract of the primitive woodland of Arden to the fringe of the teeming Meriden bypass. From the front windows of Packington Hall black fallow deer can be seen grazing in the park, and from the library at the rear the view takes in the lake and grounds laid out by 'Capability' Brown, and shaded by cedars grown from cones brought home from Lebanon. The pheasants honking proudly around have a special claim to their pride—the 4th Earl introduced the Chinese cock pheasant into England in 1770 to produce the familiar present-day bird.

It was a Herbert Fitzherbert in the thirteenth century who was first described as 'alias Finch', for he married the heiress of the Manor of Finch in Kent. The three sable griffons and a silver chevron of the Finch arms appear in many places, for they are a far-flung family, but those with whom we are concerned became the Earls of Winchelsea and Nottingham. Daniel Finch, 2nd Earl of Nottingham and 6th of Winchelsea, was a prominent politician in the reigns of James II, William III, and Anne. His long lugubrious countenance earned him the nickname of Don Dismal, and the 12 children of his second marriage, to Anne Hatton, were known as the 'Funereal Finches'. Anne's father was Governor of Guernsey, and this seems to be the slender connection with the title, Baron Guernsey, conferred on her brother-in-law Heneage Finch in 1702. Heneage was Solicitor-General until James II deprived him of the office, when he went on to become known as 'Silver-tongued' Finch for his part in the defence of the Seven Bishops in 1688. By marriage to a daughter of Sir John Banks, merchant, he obtained the Aylesford Estate in Kent.

In 1714 Baron Guernsey was created 1st Earl of Aylesford, and the earldom is one of very few without a viscountcy for its second title, the eldest son being Baron Guernsey. The titular Aylesford being in Kent, Warwickshire enters the Finch story with the marriage of the 2nd Earl of Aylesford to Mary, heiress of Sir Clement Fisher of Packington Hall, who succeeded her father in 1729—he had built the hall in 1693.

The period of the 3rd and 4th Earls, from 1757 to 1812, was one of intense building at Packington. Bonomi, a lifelong friend of the 4th Earl, built the Forest Hall in 1786, and Great Packington Church was also built during this period, started as a thanksgiving when King George III regained his sanity, but unfortunately not completed before his madness returned. Pevsner regards it as 'the most important and impressive English church of the ending eighteenth century'. It was the 4th Earl who added the two wings to Packington Hall. He was an artist with a recognizable style of his own and a member of the Royal Academy. Music was another of his interests and he installed the famous organ designed by Handel, which remained in the hall for 100 years and was removed to the church about 110 years ago.

From the 1st to the 7th Earl each had the christian name of Heneage, and the succession ran smoothly through the eldest son. The story of the 7th Earl had the theme which often evoked heart-rending fiction from Victorian novelists, that of the English aristocrat in self-imposed exile, sacrificing home and honour for someone else. He was a great friend of Edward, Prince of Wales, later Edward VII, and the expenses of a visit to Packington by the Prince nearly ruined the Aylesfords, when, among other extravagances, a ballroom was built over the entire south terrace. Ultimately his exalted friendship did ruin the 7th Earl, when he took the blame in a scandal involving the Prince of Wales, and left the country for Texas where he became known as the Cowboy Earl, dying there in 1885.

The Cowboy Earl had no male issue so the title went to his younger brother, Charles Wightwick Finch, whose heir, Heneage

Greville Finch, Baron Guernsey, was killed in action in the First World War in September 1914. His son, the 9th Earl, was killed in action at Dunkirk, so the title went back a generation to the 9th Earl's uncle, Charles Daniel Finch-Knightley, the second son of the 8th Earl, who had assumed the name of Knightley in 1912 after his grandmother's family, the Knightleys of Offchurch Bury, near Leamington Spa. It is through his second wife, Ella Victoria, that the 8th Earl has left most memories at Packington. 'Grandma was a considerable character', Lord Aylesford once told me, 'and pensioners on the estate tell wonderful tales about her. She became great friends with the stationmaster at Coventry after a right royal battle when she was shunted into a siding from the London train because she refused to travel without her two chows in the compartment.'

Like the Cowboy Earl, the 10th Earl, Lord Aylesford's father, was a case of truth being stranger than fiction. He ran away from several schools, finally going to sea before the mast. At last he got his master's certificate only to lose it because he was colour blind, so he became a lumberjack. The present Lord Aylesford succeeded to the earldom in 1958. While his cousin, the 9th Earl, was dying at Dunkirk, Lord Aylesford was serving there with the Scots Fusiliers, but was luckier in getting out unscathed. Now, in addition to playing host on many Scouting occasions, Lord Aylesford encourages country sports on his estate, with gatherings of gamekeepers, and a thriving trout fishery.

Hampton-in-Arden, three miles from Packington Park, is a pleasant dormitory village for Birmingham and Coventry, where sleep has been long disturbed by traffic on the road and in the air from Birmingham's airport at Elmdon nearby. Gone are the days, a century ago, when Sir Frederick Peel of Hampton Manor, a railway commissioner, could insist that express trains between Birmingham and Euston make a stop at Hampton-in-Arden. Some still do, but Hampton today plays a swings and roundabouts game with what is called progress, accepting the National Exhibition Centre on its doorstep and the new roads connecting with it, as the price of reducing the thunderous volume of traffic in the narrow and otherwise attractive main street. Here, for those who dare to stand and stare, is an intriguing essay in pargetting on some cottages built in 1868 by Eden Nesfield who also built the manor house.

Sir Frederick Peel was the son of Prime Minister Sir Robert Peel, and his first wife was Elizabeth Emily Shelley, a niece of the poet Percy Bysshe Shelley, which seems the sole justification for including a likeness of him, an atheist, in her memorial window in Hampton Church, along with the other writers, Langland, Chaucer, Shakespeare, Milton, Dryden, and Cowper.

The Blythe is still with us at Hampton-in-Arden, crossed by a fifteenth-century packhorse bridge of five arches. On one east pier stands the base of an ancient cross, and the letters H.B. carved on a stone indicate the boundary between Hampton and Berkswell parishes, the village of Berkswell being two miles south-eastward. The well which gives part of its name is near the church gate, a large stoutly-constructed stone tank which could have been used for immersion at baptisms. Nearby, the stocks repay close inspection—they have an odd number of ankle-holes—five—and tradition has it that a confirmed local malefactor had only one leg.

Berkswell Church has a Norman nave arcade, a Norman door with a timber porch which has an upper storey accessible by an exterior staircase, and a Norman crypt with an architecturally mysterious octagonal western extension. A rare south gallery and box pews add to the church's attractions. There is some good newish carving in the choir where, in addition to SS. Chad, Wulstan, and Dunstan, there are Hugh Latimer, one-time Bishop of Worcester who was burned at the stake in Mary Tudor's reign, and Robert de Lymesley. Outside, just east of the porch, stands a slate headstone to a 20-year-old youth who died of a broken heart—'Deceived by one I lov'd, I lov'd most dear'.

The sixteenth-century Bear Inn at Berkswell has, among other attractions, a gun captured from the Russians at Kertch in the Crimea on 5 May 1855 by Captain Arthur E. Wilmot. It was fired outside the 'Bear' on 4 January 1859 followed by a dinner for which the local gentry paid 3s. 6d. each.

Despite the constant erosion of the countryside by road and house building it is possible, even between Birmingham and Coventry, to find pleasant walks by lane and fieldpath. Once a week I do the same 10½ mile circular walk from Knowle, only four miles from the south-east boundary of Birmingham. A mile of the Kenilworth road from Knowle Church takes me past old cottages bearing fire-marks—metal insurance plates—and across the Birmingham-Warwick Canal where pleasure boats cluster above Knowle Locks, to Cuttle Pool Lane. From the bridge where the Cuttle Brook hurries down to the River Blythe I regularly see a kingfisher, a heron, and large chub down below. Squirrels and rabbits abound behind Chadwick Manor, the bullfinch has ousted the chaffinch, and in Sparrowcock Lane snipe jink away from marshy fields. For some years on this walk I have watched the diligent Miss Ann Moore in her father's fields jumping her way to the proud title she won in 1971 of European Women's Show Jumping Champion. Horses clip-clop along these lanes, too, and on Sunday mornings parents in large cars convey their solemn-faced and appropriately-accoutred offspring to a riding stable, children who would be better occupied walking the lanes than seeking status on horseback.

But this is horse country. I watched the conversion week after week of an old cottage until eventually a name went up in gold lettering on a yoke—'Town Crier Cottage'. My enquiries revealed that Town Crier was the most successful horse of the young wife at the cottage, herself a well-known local horsewoman. Any point of my walk is likely to be rendered suddenly raucous by the braying of a donkey. To have a donkey in the paddock seems almost an equivalent status symbol to having a Jaguar in the garage, and donkeys today are thick in Warwickshire pastures. At Claverdon, near Henley-in-Arden, there is a busy donkey stud.

My return route to Knowle takes me, in Temple Balsall, down the charming backwater of Bread Walk. Here is the Lady Catherine Leveson Hospital, founded in 1677 by a granddaughter of Robert Dudley, Earl of Leicester, a sunny haven for old ladies whose original red brick almshouses line either side of an oblong courtyard closed at the far end by the Master's House, built in 1836, with two towers, one with a clock, the other with a sundial. Beside the hospital is Temple Balsall Church, built originally in 1290 by the Military Order of Knights Templars, on whose suppression it passed to the Knights Hospitallers. Only one mile away is a Saracen's Head Inn, often to be found in the vicinity of a centre of the Templars who fought against the Infidel in the Crusades. In 1662 Lady Catherine and her sister, Lady Anne Holbourne, restored the church which had lost its roof. Sir Gilbert Scott effected a restoration in the mid-nineteenth century, and today no church in Warwickshire fits more felicitously into its picturesque surroundings.

The multitude of corbels is a fascinating feature—knights, bishops and kings inside, and their cheery or lugubrious retainers outside, their dogs clinging to the buttresses high on the red sandstone ashlar walls. Lofty, the chancel as large as the nave, with no chancel arch or protuberances, the austere interior can be seen at a glance, ascending from west to east with a deliberate lack of symmetry; no two windows alike or quite opposite, no ledges at the same height. The dreadful west window has a rose window above it. The east window is both attractive and purposeful, with SS. Augustine and Oswald of Worcester, a Templar and a Hospitaller, their heraldic arms, and those of the Holbourne sisters who rebuilt the church.

A walnut tree among the churchyard yews casts its shade on the rows of little headstones where the old ladies from the hospital lie, and their graves have overflowed to the newer churchyard across the stream. Here, as you come up the path from Bread Walk, you are confronted by a story unexpected in Warwickshire. Immediately facing the path is the memorial stone of Henry Williams who died in 1924—author of 'It's a long long way to Tipperary'—the great marching song of the Kaiser's War. Two miles distant, at Meer End, stands the Tipperary Inn, with a bar of the music as its sign. It was there, when the pub was kept by Williams's uncle and known as the 'Plough' before 1914, that Henry, with his friend and fellow-entertainer, Jack Judge, composed the famous song, Williams the music, Judge the words. Controversy has raged about the origin of Tipperary, but it seems likely that, at first, it was a long way to Connemara. It was at the Grand Theatre, Stalybridge, Cheshire, in 1912, that Judge gave the song its first public performance, but substituted Tipperary for Connemara.

Knowle Church, battlemented and beautifully lit by clerestory windows, is dedicated to SS. John the Baptist, Lawrence, and Anne, all appearing in small reliefs on the façade of the fifteenth-century timber Guild House alongside. Among many interesting windows, one in the soldiers' chapel could well be unique in quoting VIII Corps Orders of 4 July 1916, referring to the Warwickshire Regiment at Beaumont Hamel in the battle on 1 July: 'There were no cowards or waverers, and not a man fell out. It was a magnificent display of disciplined courage worthy of the best traditions of the British race'. Above the pulpit is an hour glass for the timing of sermons.

Knowle's main street has been described recently as a 'film set' —all Tudor whimsy on the façade. Quite authentic is Grimshaw Hall, E-shaped in compliment to Queen Elizabeth in whose reign it was built, black and white, timbered and many-gabled.

Telford in Warwickshire? Surely not—yet the workaday name of Shropshire's new town was once bestowed by the Rev. W. H. Hinder, curate of neighbouring Barston in his novel *The Curate of Rigg*, on respectable residential Solihull, the *'Urbs in Rure'* on Birmingham's south-eastern border. Solihull, always the butt of inverted 'Brummie' snobs as a genteel 'curtains and kippers' community, has taken some knocks of recent years, with noisy youth clubs, a growing 'pop' tradition, all-in wrestling in the fine new Civic Hall, the constant industrial disputes at the Rover Car Company, and, as I write, the inheritance in the boundary reshuffle of Birmingham's vast slum clearance township, Chelmsley Wood.

Motorists curse Solihull for its three pairs of traffic lights on the Warwick Road, lights that encourage speeding and breath-taking and amber jumping even by so timid a motorist as I am.

In these same eyes Solihull's proudest possession is Solihull School, which has retained so much that is traditional from the better days of the public school. One word, however, you will seek in vain— prefect. The Solihull equivalent is bencher. Care must be taken with terminology, too, saying Head of the School and Head of the House, not School or House Captain; and Captain of the Fifteen or Captain of the Eleven for rugger or cricket, but Captain of hockey, swimming or shooting.

Though some suggest that 1381 may be the year of its founda-tion, it is more likely that Solihull School is contemporary with the Edward vi foundations, and 1560 is generally accepted. In that year the revenue of the Chantry Chapels of St. Katherine and St. Mary in Solihull Church were diverted for the school's endowment, and to them were added in 1566 the revenues of the Chantry of St. Alphege. Solihull Church is dedicated to the obscure Alphege, Arch-bishop of Canterbury, whose martyrdom by the Danes is depicted in a window. His association with Solihull arises from his having been Bishop of Worcester in which diocese Solihull was before Birmingham became a bishopric.

Abounding in the church, particularly among the hatchments on the south nave wall, is the coat-of-arms with two greyhounds of the great family of Solihull, the Greswolds, who built Malvern Hall in the eighteenth century. A David Lewis lived there subsequently, and among Solihull's hatchments are those of two of his daughters —each a Countess of Dysart, a Scottish earldom. Magdalene was the second wife of the fifth earl and her sister, Anna Maria, was wife of the sixth earl. So, as her husband predeceased Magdalene, she was Dowager Countess of Dysart while her sister was the extant Countess—not bad for the family of a commoner.

You search Domesday Book in vain for Solihull. The area was in the Manor of Ulverley, a name which declined as Solihull grew nearby, leaving Ulverley the Old Town, ultimately Olton. Henry VI appointed Thomas Greswold custodian of the Manor of Solihull, but the family association with the manor lasted only seven years. In Tudor times a Greswold built Solihull Manor House, though this was not a manor house in the sense of being the home of the lords of the manor. This Manor House survives today, a charming black and white intrusion in the modern High Street, run by a trust, and the meeting place of some 50 Solihull organizations.

Sandalls Bridge carries the Warwick road out of Solihull across the Blythe. It is named after an absentee rector of Solihull, John de Sandale, Chancellor of England to Edward II and Chancellor of the Exchequer also. Between Knowle and Warwick, in leafy Arden parkland, stands Wroxall Abbey School for girls. Within the grounds of the mansion built by the Dugdales in 1868 stands St. Leonard's, Wroxall parish church and the school chapel in one, and every Ascension Morning the school choir sings hymns from the tower. The school moved in from Rugby in 1936, but Wroxall Abbey has a history dating back to the early fourteenth century which is recorded in a beautiful stained-glass window above the front staircase.

Sir Hewe de Hatton, taken prisoner on a Crusade, dreams of St. Leonard, patron of prisoners. Miraculously the saint transports Sir Hewe to Wroxall Wood, where his wife accepts him only on his producing half the ring they broke on parting. In thanksgiving they found a Benedictine Priory on the spot, dedicating it to St. Leonard. Around 1315 the Virgin Mary appears to Prioress Alice Craft and bids her build the church which still stands—this is the story in the window.

Henry VIII dissolved the priory, and its buildings were partly incorporated in a mansion built by Robert Burgoyne. In 1713 Sir Christopher Wren purchased it on his son's marriage to Sir Roger Burgoyne's widow, though all that remains with certainty of the great architect is the serpentine garden wall. The mansion was eventually demolished and the existing house built by the Warwickshire Dugdales in 1868. All three families are lavishly commemorated in the church, including five Christopher Wrens who followed their famous forebear. The excellent east window features St. Benedict and his sister St. Scholastica, St. Leonard with his fetters, and St. Edmund. Beneath the cypresses and cedars overhanging the priory ruins, a dogs' cemetery has intruded in the roofless chapter house.

West of the Warwick road a tract of lovely country stretches to, and beyond, the Stratford road. It is cut by the Grand Union Canal and the southern section of the Stratford Canal which was taken over by the National Trust in 1964 and re-opened to pleasure boats, though it makes a fine walk, too. Its particular features are the barrel-roofed lock cottages and the cantilever 'nick bridges', so called from the gap which enabled the tow rope to follow the horse when the tow-path changed sides of the canal. At Preston Bagot the red brick and timber manor house invites the canal navigator to reach for his camera, while at Lowsonford the canalside pub, the 'Fleur-de-Lys' gave its name to pies made there, which have become famous. They are now produced beside another canal, the Grand Union at Emscote, Warwick, where tribute is paid to them in the name of the nearby pub, the 'Simple Simon'.

Yarningale Common, beside the Stratford Canal south of Lowsonford, is also a gastronomic memory to Midland ramblers, who have crowded into Mrs. Sheath's cottage for many years to consume enormous teas, while she had to be forced to increase her charges with the rising cost of living. The canal crosses the Stratford road at Wootten Wawen, continuing to Bearley which has another long and impressive aqueduct.

In the early years of last century, when the 'navvies' constructing the canal navigations were a lawless bunch, the Tanworth Association for the Prosecution of Felons was formed, based on Tanworth-in-Arden, near the Stratford Canal. Its purpose long since done, the association still exists as a social institution, and it serves to introduce a famous Arden family by recording that as many as 30 Burmans once attended a single Felons gathering. Another Felons association, which did not survive, was started at Hockley Heath, Hockley Port as it was known, with its salt warehouse on the canal behind the Wharf Inn.

Among the 'preservation' stickers which proliferate in car windows, 'Save the Tapster Valley' has had an excellent showing over the past two years. Named after an obscure brook, the 'valley', threatened with a thoroughly needless motorway, runs through sylvan country between Lowsonford and Lapworth, where there is a church of outstanding interest, with a detached tower joined by a modern vestibule to the nave, and an upper room at the west end which may once have held a relic. By some coincidence the War Memorial Chapel was rebuilt in the fifteenth century by the Catesby family of Bushwood, and dedicated to St. Catherine of Antioch, whose attribute is the spiked wheel on which she was tortured. This has given its name to the firework, the Catherine Wheel, and it was Robert Catesby of the Bushwood family who was the leading conspirator in the Gunpowder Plot which has given us Bonfire Night.

Not two miles westward, the Nuthurst Obelisk was raised in 1749 by Thomas Archer, architect of St. Philip's Cathedral, Birmingham, to celebrate his elevation to the peerage. From his home, Umberslade Park, a long avenue leads to Tanworth-in-Arden, a picture-postcard village with the 'Bell' and the church set off by a chestnut tree where the street widens. Tanworth Church offers much to the hagiologist. One window has three northern saints, Columba, Magnus, and Olave; and among many more saints we find Martin, a soldier holding a sword and the cloak he shared with a naked beggar. When Bishop Gore dedicated this window he was critical of the saint's unsoldierly stance.

Six miles south-eastward, not even its traffic can destroy the charm of Henley-in-Arden's long High Street, into which the church tower protrudes about half-way, a pleasing background to the vista

whether seen from the 'Black Swan' or the 'Golden Cross'. North
of the church the tree-lined greater width and an ancient cross give
particular character to the street. Henley is famous for its ice cream
and its December turkey market; less so for its Court Leet and its
Guildhall; while the village novelist is practically forgotten. He was
Keble Howard, son of a vicar of Henley, the Rev. G. E. Bell, and
two at least of his novels were set locally: *The Happy Vanners*, a
story of gipsies, and *The God in the Garden*. He called Henley
Wootton-in-Arden, and the Alne the Sling. There is a footpath
beside the River Alne at the back of the houses on the east side of
High Street, many of the gardens having bridges across the river
to the path.

Beside Henley Church a road leads across the river to Beaudesert
Church, and, not a quarter of a mile apart, the two must be the
nearest church neighbours in Warwickshire. Dedicated to St.
Nicholas, Beaudesert Church has an appealing weather vane showing the saint with the three children he saved from a frying-vat.
A splendid Norman south door introduces the visitor to other Norman features, and the gate beside the churchyard wall gives access
to the hill fortified by the Norman de Montforts with a motte-and-
bailey castle, only the earthworks of which remain. From them it is a
pleasant view across the jumble of ancient roofs with the two
church towers—less pleasant if one looks farther afield and takes
in the new building that has half encircled Henley in the past decade.
Two miles of field paths provide an enjoyable walk from Henley to
Preston Bagot.

South of Henley, at Wootton Wawen, the Alne foams down a
weir beneath the Stratford road bridge, the parapet of which incorporates a milestone dated 1806, reading 'To London, 100 miles'.
It is known that the Prince Regent, later George iv, used often to
sigh and wish he was a hundred miles from London—for at Wootton
Hall beside the Alne lived the twice-widowed Mrs. Maria Fitzherbert,
whom the prince was to marry clandestinely in 1785. In the
Boudoir Bedroom at Wootton Hall the Prince of Wales feathers
are a reminder of this liaison, as is also the motto on the beautiful
coat-of-arms adorning a pediment above the entrance. '*Regi semper
fidelis*' it reads—'Always faithful to the King', as indeed Maria was,
for she genuinely loved George.

But the arms and motto are those of the 1st Viscount Carington
—a Smith of Wootton Wawen; four peacocks with a red cross
between them. The Smiths' loyalty was to Charles I who created
Sir Charles Smith Viscount Carington in 1643. In 1665 Carington
was murdered by his valet in France, but his heart was brought back
to Wootton Hall. Captain Hubert Berkeley, who lived at the hall
as a child a century ago wrote in 1937: 'The Carington heart was
in an old heart-shaped oak box lined with velvet. Mr. William
Keyte found it in a cupboard ... not knowing what to do with it,
he put it in a grave when he was burying someone in the Catholic
cemetery'. There, presumably, it lies today, between the river and
the canal aqueduct.

A pack of bloodhounds is hunted from Wootton Hall; there is a
residential caravan site at the rear, and beyond it, on an islet in a
lake, a populous heronry. Hereabouts, too, are the osier beds from
which John Gardner so long made his hurdles.

One is hard put to find any orthodox pattern in the interior of
Wootton Wawen Church, but it incorporates an Anglo-Saxon central
tower. Among memorials to the gentry, there is a verse by the
Rev. J. Gaches to John Hoitt, huntsman to the poet, William Somerville, which begins:

> *Here Hoitt, all his sports and labours past*
> *Joins his loved master, Somerville, at last.*

Somerville was one of the literary coterie which gathered around
Henrietta, Lady Luxborough, at Barrells Hall, two miles west of
Henley-in-Arden, in a country of winding lanes around Ullenhall,
Oldberrow, and Morton Bagot, where the timber-turreted church
is a hidden gem, still with candle sconces for lighting. Ullenhall's
old church, St. Mary's, is even more off the beaten track, merely
the chancel of the original church, but with fascinating memorials.
There is a lengthy epitaph—or so it seems—to Sir Francis Throckmorton, but it turns out to be that shabby trick of using one person's memorial to eulogize another, in this case, Francis's father,
Michael. He lived in Italy 'in good and great reputation with bounti-
ful hospitality entertaining most of the noblemen and gentlemen
of England that had occasion to come that way'. The inscription

goes on to say that Michael returned to England in Mary Tudor's reign 'and received of her the gift of the manors of Honiley, Blackwell, Packhurst, Winderton, and Ullenhall'. It omits even to mention the death of poor Francis.

Lady Luxborough (1699-1756) lies in a vault at St. Mary's. Through conduct which she herself described as 'more than prudence or decency allows' with a minor poet, Dalton, she was separated from her husband. He allowed her to remain at Barrells where a group of lesser literary figures centred around her, including the poets Jago, Somerville, and Shenstone. By the terms of the separation Lady Luxborough was not allowed to leave England nor go within 20 miles of London. She lived, however, in some style at Barrells, being constantly chided by her husband for living beyond her allowance.

A difficult half-mile path may be followed from St. Mary's to Hall End Farm, isolated in the fields with its grim story. One day in 1808, William Booth of Perry Barr, visiting the farm, was supposed to have killed his brother John with a shovel, though William was acquitted, the injuries being put down to kicks from a horse. Four years later William Booth's home at Perry Barr was found to be the headquarters of a thriving forgery industry—a capital crime for which William was sentenced to death. He went to the gallows at Stafford Gaol, was pinioned, blindfolded, and the rope placed round his neck. The hangman then pulled the lever. The trap opened and Booth disappeared—but so did the rope which they had omitted to secure to the gallows. Like a sack Booth fell the 12 feet of the drop and knocked himself out. So they revived him and replaced him on the scaffold, but now the mechanism went wrong, and the unfortunate forger had three times to give the sign with his handkerchief before he was successfully hanged.

In 1963 the farmer at Hall End told me of his five-year plan to reduce 13 fields to four by removing hedges—a general tendency today, for a hedgerow can waste a strip ten yards wide.

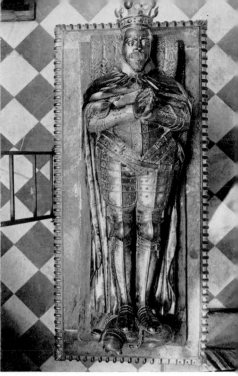

25 Coleshill's Norman font

26 Ambrose Dudley, Earl of War-
wick, died 21 February 1589,
Beauchamp Chapel, St.
Mary's, Warwick

27 A misericord from Holy Trinity Church, Stratford-upon-Avon

CHAPTER NINE

Rugby and the Upper Avon

Dunchurch, a mile inside Warwickshire from the Northamptonshire boundary on the Rains Brook, is one of England's lucky villages —saved from its insupportable burden of traffic by the M45 feeder to the M1 Motorway. There has been new building, but 'Alpha and Omega Villas, 1884' still show where first you entered or last you left the village on the A45. Dunchurch stands at the eastern fringe of Dunsmore Heath, no longer recognizable as such by motorists hurtling along the A45, but once a wilderness roamed by the legendary Dun Cow, slain eventually by Guy of Warwick, and later the haunt of highwaymen.

On 5 November 1605 a hundred horsemen enjoyed a hunt on Dunsmore Heath, and thronged into the Lion Inn, Dunchurch, for supper. They were the leading Catholic gentry of the Midlands, ready to seize Princess Elizabeth, daughter of James I, from Coombe Abbey, near Coventry, and place her on the throne on hearing of Guy Fawkes having successfully blown up the king, his sons, and Parliament in the Gunpowder Plot. But Robert Catesby, the arch plotter, having spurred 80 miles from London in seven hours, disrupted the meal with news of Guy Fawkes's failure and arrest.

Nevertheless Catesby still called on the party at the 'Lion' to rise in revolt, but wiser spirits realized the futility of this and left. The hundred dwindled to 40, and these diehards set out towards Worcestershire and Wales, hoping to recruit Catholics to their cause en route. At midnight they stole some horses at Warwick; then on, four miles more, to 'Norbrook', John Grant's house near Snitterfield, to collect weapons before continuing westward at daybreak.

Speeding through Great Alne and Arrow, the conspirators bypassed Coughton Court, where some of their womenfolk had gathered, and rode out of Warwickshire to ultimate death or capture at Holbeche House, near Dudley.

What was once the 'Lion' in Dunchurch is now known as Guy Fawkes House, a row of dwellings half-timbered and well-preserved, the first floor protruding over a raised cobbled path. With the church, the 'Green Man' on the inn sign leaping among exploding crackers, and trees on a green, it forms an attractive village centrepiece, presided over by a large statue of Lord John Douglas Montagu Douglas Scott, third son of the fourth Duke of Buccleuch. Why is this scion of a Scottish dukedom commemorated thus in Warwickshire?

The king was Lord of the Manor of Knightlow hereabouts until 1629 when Charles I gave the lordship to Sir Francis Leigh, who became Baron Dunsmore and Earl of Chichester. His daughter Elizabeth succeeded him, and the lordship of Knightlow went to the Montagu family of Boughton, Northamptonshire, when her daughter, also Elizabeth, took as her second husband Ralph Montagu, created Duke of Montagu in 1707. Dying in 1709 he was succeeded by his son John who became a great planter of trees in his park at Boughton and on his Warwickshire estate around Dunchurch. In 1740 he planted six miles of an avenue from Stretton-on-Dunsmore to Dunchurch and beyond, hoping to continue it to London. These activities earned him the description 'John the Planter', a name sometimes wrongly attributed to Lord John Scott. The Planter died in 1749 and his younger daughter, Mary, inherited his estates. In 1766 the dukedom was revived for her husband, George Brudenell, fourth Earl of Cardigan, on whose death the estates went to his daughter, yet another Elizabeth. By marrying Henry Scott, third Duke of Buccleuch, she brought the Buccleuchs to the Midlands, and on her death in 1827 her Warwickshire estate and the lordship of the Manor of Knightlow devolved upon her grandson, Lord John Scott— he of the Dunchurch statue.

It was to Cawston House, Dunchurch, that Lord John took his bride in 1836. She was Alicia Ann Spottiswoode from Berwickshire, a name which means nothing nowadays though most of us are still familiar with her work. She composed the air to 'Annie Laurie', published in 1838, and to her is also attributed the tune of 'The Bonnie Banks of Loch Lomond'. Cawston House still stands, the research centre of an engineering group. Alicia and her husband became much loved as benefactors in Dunchurch, though they ruled with a rod of iron. Lord John was a trustee of Rugby School and a pillar of the church in his village. In 1841 he had the seating of St. Peter's entirely renewed on the open system, doing away with private box pews and asking 'just a space where I may sit among the labouring men of the parish.'

His lands and sway extended to Newnham Regis, three miles north-westward of Dunchurch, where a church tower stands in the farm-yard of Newnham Hall Farm. The church was demolished in 1795, and in 1852 his lordship decided to clear the site. Doing so, he unearthed several coffins. One contained the skeleton of a male who had been beheaded—the skull lying away from the neck. The only identification with these grisly remains were the initials T.B. on some faded clothing. Two other coffins were those of Francis Leigh, the aforementioned Earl of Chichester, who died in 1653, and his countess. A fourth was that of their young daughter, Lady Audrey Leigh, who died in 1640, and she lay embalmed in her leaden coffin, beautiful and perfectly preserved after 212 years. Lord John had the coffins replaced in a vault, having provided the daughter with a fine brass in her likeness and bearing the words: 'Here is inclosed the body of Mrs. Audrey Leigh, eldest daughter of Francis, Lord Dunsmore, died 28 January 1640.'

Walking once through Newnham Regis, I called at Newnham Hall Farm and asked if there were any remains to be seen of the old church. From indoors the farmer produced Audrey Leigh's brass, and told me that, investigating the sudden disappearance of a pool in his farmyard, he had discovered a vault below with seven leaden coffins.

Lord John Scott died on 3 January 1860, and the statue was erected 'by his tenantry in affectionate remembrance of him.' Alicia was 90 when she died in 1900. A plaque to Lord John above the choir in St. Peter's Church bears the text 'Lead me to a rock that is higher than I,' and on a pew end the three legs of Man are a reminder that a fifteenth-century vicar, John Grene, held the living of Dunchurch in plurality with the Bishopric of Sodor and Man.

The lordship of the Manor of Knightlow still rests with the Duke of Buccleuch, and thereby hangs one of Warwickshire's most interesting customs—the Wroth Silver ceremony enacted before sunrise each 11 November at Knightlow Hill, Stretton-on-Dunsmore. It is a four-mile journey from Dunchurch, along the A45, passing the motorway roundabout, the new reservoir of Draycote Water with its trout fishing, a Blue Boar Farm, the monolith commemorating the review by King George v on 12 March 1915 of the 29th Division before it embarked for Gallipoli, and two Dun Cow inns.

The second of these, at Stretton-on-Dunsmore, is an unexpected scene of activity before daybreak every 11 November, with lights blazing, doors hospitably open, and license operating. 'What is it, mate?' a passing lorry driver asked me in 1967, 'a demonstration against the breathalyser?' He nipped in for a drink to prove that it was all happening, and then followed the throng along the road, through a gate, and to a stone trough, the hollow base of an ancient cross on a grassy mound. While a hundred gathered around, two men removed their hats, and one raised his voice. He was the agent for the Duke of Buccleuch, who does not himself attend.

'Wroth Silver', he began, 'collected annually at Knightlow Cross by His Grace the Duke of Buccleuch as Lord of the Manor of the Hundred of Knightlow. Arley, one penny; Astley, one penny; Birdingbury, one penny....' At each call someone stepped forward and a coin clinked into the trough.

'What is it—three coins in the fountain?' the mystified lorry driver asked.

The list continued until the names of 25 parishes had been called and representatives of each had thrown in sums mainly up to 4d, but with Leamington Hastings 1s.; Long Itchington 2s. 2d.; and Harbury 2s. 3½d., bringing the total to 9s. 4d. As each person throws his parish levy into the trough he says 'Wroth Silver'. The entire ceremony is unofficial, with private individuals, some of whom have attended for 50 years; a Rover crew; a British Legion branch, coming forward just to preserve the tradition. The penalty for non-payment is a 20s. fine for every penny—or the forfeiture of a white bull with red ears and nose, a descendant of the original wild cattle of Britain.

The money collected, the party returns to the Dun Cow Inn for breakfast, and, in the words of Victor Neal, the Wroth Silver laureate:

And rum and milk, if one so care
To quench the frosty touch in air,
One custom more, must now evoke
Churchwarden pipes for us to smoke.

The 1970 ceremony was the 780th annual collection of Wroth
Silver, so it has seen sufficient changes in currency not to be worried
by decimalization. As to the origin of Wroth Silver there are several
possibilities, the most likely suggesting a medieval road tax paid
to the Lord of the Hundred for keeping the roads of the day in
good repair. The Anglo-Saxon 'word'—pronounced 'worth' means
a roadway. 'Weordi' is a field, and also means 'price'. Pronounced
as 'weorth' it is easily corruptible to 'wroth'. 'Rother heyder' or
cattle money, a grazing fee, is another alternative origin. 'Ward
money' in lieu of military service, or 'wrath money' levied against
the Hundred for the murder of someone of consequence—these are
other conjectures.

The A45 was Telford's coach road from London to Holyhead,
and at Stretton-on-Dunsmore it is crossed by the Roman Fosse Way.
Northward in the steps of the Legions for a mile, a turn left, and
we are in Wolston. With Haseley Manor, near Warwick, and White
Friars, Coventry, Wolston Priory shares the distinction of having
housed the printing presses from which, in the late sixteenth century, John Penry, a pioneer of Welsh non-conformity, published
his bitingly satirical Martin Marprelate Tracts against the Church,
and, in particular, against the bishops. He was hanged in 1593 for
incitement to rebellion.

Crossing the Avon and continuing north from Wolston, we come
within three miles by a bridle path through New Close Wood—to
Coombe Park, Pool, and Abbey, where, you will recall, young Princess Elizabeth was lodged at the time of the Gunpowder Plot. You
cannot get more scornful than to say 'It isn't worth a brass farthing',
yet the education and upbringing of this princess were paid for in
brass farthings; at least in a grant to mint brass farthings. The man
who received the grant was Lord Harington of Coombe Abbey, host,
faithful guardian and tutor to Princess Elizabeth. Making the grant
was her father, James I, who so far forgot his Scots canniness as to
bankrupt himself in paying for Elizabeth's wedding in 1613 to

Frederick, the Elector Palatine. Thus he could not afford the £30,000 he had promised Lord Harington for bringing up the princess. Hence the brass farthings.

Since the City of Coventry opened Coombe Abbey as a recreation area in 1966 children have romped among the magnificent woodlands and lakeside groves where Elizabeth grew up far from the intrigues and dangers of her father's Court. Lord Harington had, in fact, received advance warning of the Gunpowder Plotters' intentions to kidnap his charge, so had hurried her into the safety of Old Palace Yard, Coventry. Returning to Coombe Abbey when the danger was over, and told of the plot to put her on the throne, she made the mature and filial observation: 'I would sooner have died with my father than have come to the throne in such a fashion.'

Coombe Abbey had come to Lord Harington with his wife, Elizabeth Kelway, daughter of a lawyer who bought the property from the Crown to which it had reverted when John, Earl of Warwick and Duke of Northumberland, was executed for the treason of placing his daughter-in-law, Lady Jane Grey, on Mary Tudor's throne. Northumberland had been granted Coombe Abbey at the Dissolution of the Monasteries. Founded in 1150, it was one of three great Cistercian houses in Warwickshire, the others being Stoneleigh and Merevale. The cloisters still remain at Coombe, though the only surviving fragment of the twelfth-century building is a red sandstone ashlar doorway, the entrance in monastic days to the chapter house. It leads now to a refreshment counter, with seats for trippers where once the white-habited monks took their exercise.

After Princess Elizabeth's marriage Lord Harington accompanied her to her new home at Heidelberg. On his way home he died, followed soon by his son and heir, so Coombe Abbey descended to his daughter, Lucy, whose extravagance brought about the sale of the abbey in 1622 to Elizabeth, Lady Craven. With her son, William, the first Earl Craven, Coombe Abbey again impinged on the life of Elizabeth who, with her husband, had ascended the throne of Bohemia in 1619, and given birth to a son who became the famous Prince Rupert of the English Civil War. Craven befriended her when she returned to England in 1661, a widow, and his London house became her home. It was even suggested that they married, but definite proof is lacking. When she died next year Elizabeth left her big collection of pictures to Craven. The earldom, though not a barony, died with his son, but there was a second creation in 1801. Meanwhile five more barons had lived successively at Coombe Abbey. William, the sixth Lord Craven, born in 1738, was the son of the Rev. John Craven, Vicar of Stanton Lacy, Shropshire, only five miles from Craven Arms which takes its name from the family.

At Coombe Abbey the grounds were landscaped by 'Capability' Brown. With the biggest natural lake in Warwickshire, and the magnificent wellingtonias now having reached maturity. Coventry has a splendid recreational asset. Two Earls of Craven became Lords-Lieutenant of Warwickshire, and they are commemorated in Craven Arms hotels at Binley, Southam, and Coventry. Coombe Abbey remained in the family until 1923. Three Earls of Craven have died since 1921 with a consequent drain on the family resources for death duties, so, in 1968, the Craven Collection of paintings was sold at Sotheby's for £263,880. Included were many of Elizabeth's pictures, one of herself raising £5,200 and one of Frederick £4,600. Thus it was that three centuries after the Cravens befriended her in adversity Elizabeth of Bohemia—the 'Winter Queen' as she was known—paid her debt to the family.

Coombe Abbey has brought us to the eastern perimeter of Coventry, but westward bland pastures spread beside the Avon for seven miles towards Rugby. In this valley, around King's Newnham, we catch sight of the spires of Rugby, but there is a story to detain us before we reach this seat of learning and industry.

Half a mile east of King's Newnham a cottage beside the Avon was once a spa, a small one, but with waters specific against 'the stone, green wounds, ulcers, and imposthumes' according to a seventeenth-century book. Two stone troughs in the garden, and an old bath house, are all the remaining signs of the spa, said to have been recommended to Queen Elizabeth 1 by her physician, and actually visited by Queen Anne. Had the Dowager Lady Boughton of Lawford Hall and her daughter Theodosia been content to 'take the waters' at Newnham Spa, just down the road from their home in June 1777 a tragedy might have been averted. Instead they preferred the brighter lights and polite society of Bath, where they met Captain John Donnellan of the 39th Regiment. Theodosia was infatuated by him and ultimately the pair eloped. The Boughton family was enraged, but when Donnellan repudiated any share in his wife's fortune he was accepted at Lawford Hall.

In the summer of 1780 Theodosia's brother, Sir Theodosius Boughton, Bart., came down from Eton to take up life as squire of Lawford. He was a debauched young man, and though he used Donnellan to extricate him from various scrapes he hated his brother-in-law. Donnellan, for his part, seems to have had homicidal ideas, for he began talking about the precarious state of Theodosius's health, and warned Theodosia against drinking from her brother's cups as he sometimes mixed rat poison.

On the night of 29 August 1780 Donnellan showed concern lest the young baronet should catch cold while fishing. Next morning Lady Boughton gave her son a draught of medicine prepared by a Rugby doctor. Remarking that it tasted unduly bitter, Sir Theodosius lay down, went into convulsions, and was obviously dying. Returning home, Donnellan inspected the medicine bottle and aroused Lady Boughton's suspicion by washing it. When a doctor arrived Theodosius was dead, and was duly buried. But at the prompting of Lord Denbigh and the Vicar of Newbold there was an exhumation, the body was opened, and an acrid smell of laurel water detected.

On 14 September a coroner's jury found Donnellan guilty of wilful murder. The trial at Warwick on 30 March 1781 found that Sir Theodosius had died through drinking laurel water, at which, in a book of Donnellan's a page was turned down. Sentenced to death, the captain was hanged at Warwick on 2 April 1781. Theodosia remarried twice, first Sir Egerton Leigh, and then Barry O'Meara, a surgeon who attended Napoleon on St. Helena, though it is as Dame Theodosia Beauchamp that she is described in Newbold Church where she lies with Sir Egerton. She assumed the name of Beauchamp after Donnellan's execution.

Newbold Church, east of the site of Lawford Hall which was demolished ten years after the murder, is a monument to the Boughtons. Beneath an engraved slab lie Thomas and Elizabeth, a fifteenth-century couple. The sixteenth century is represented most picturesquely by Edward and Elizabeth with their progeny on a wall monument. But the doyen of the family was a Boughton who was

Vicar of Newbold for 50 years, dying in 1902 aged 79. He rejoiced —if it were cause for rejoicing—in the name of the Rev. Theodosius Edgerton B. W. Boughton-Leigh. Another line of note in the ministry at Newbold—the Parkers—provided three John Parkers as vicars in succession from 1742 to 1852.

Rugby, for all its population of 60,000, its major electrical, cement, and other industries, and its importance as a railway junction, is first and foremost Rugby School, and the town is a poorer place since the boys were 'emancipated' from those multi-coloured school caps as they hurried between their formrooms, boarding houses, and other establishments such as the Temple Reading Room and Art School. Armfuls of books still identify the boys, but their garb is more heterogeneous even than that of their neighbours at Lawrence Sheriff School, who do wear uniform sports jackets.

Sheriff, who made the name of Rugby synonymous with learning, was born at Rugby or Brownsover nearby, and became a London grocer of sufficient standing to receive a grant of arms from Elizabeth I. As a servant of the palace, probably a tradesman by appointment, he was allowed to add a fleur-de-lys and two Tudor roses to his own three griffin's heads. Today his coat of arms, with the motto *'Orando Laborando'* (By prayer and work) is world famous as the badge of Rugby School, but it is from the façade of Lawrence Sheriff School, opened in 1878, that in fur-lined cloak and Tudor cap, the London grocer looks out across Clifton Road.

Married but childless, at his death in 1567 he left the rents of property in Rugby and Brownsover, together with one third of his Middlesex estate, to provide for the education of boys in Rugby. Rugby School was established at once, and, with Sheriff's endowment proving so profitable, it was able to set up boarding houses which attracted a richer class of pupil from all over Britain. This was not quite the founder's intention, and it was Dr. William Temple, later Archbishop of Canterbury, who, during his headship of Rugby School, persuaded the governors of the need for a school to cater for town boys. Today Lawrence Sheriff's School's impact on Rugby town is greater than that of the more famous school which draws its boarders from far and wide so that they disperse after their schooldays.

The most ancient of Rugby School's buildings have a fine façade on Lawrence Sheriff Street, enhanced by a tower gateway. Turning into Barby Road, the visitor can walk between the headmaster's house and the green acres of the Close with its playing fields to the very heart of Rugby School—its chapel, rebuilt by Butterfield after the 1867 tercentenary, with a splendid octagonal tower 105 feet tall. In the Doctor's Wall to the right a plaque commemorates William Webb Ellis 'who with a fine disregard for the rules of football as played in his time first took the ball in his arms and ran with it, thus originating the distinctive feature of the Rugby game, A.D. 1823.'

During the 1914-18 War the Christmas card sent by Rugby School to Old Rugbeians on active service bore a picture of the school chapel, with the words: 'The chapel bell rings at noon each day, when all work stops and we think of you and wish you well.' So much was Rugby Chapel the focus of the school, and to Rugbeians today it is still the heart of their community.

You enter by the war memorial chapel, built in honour of 628 Rugbeians who fell in the First World War—nearly one in four of those who served. To their names, enshrined in its walls, are added the dead in 1939-45, bare of rank or honours, though Rugby had four V.C.s in the 1914-18 War. Leaving the chapel on your right you go ahead through two more doors into the west end of Rugby Chapel proper, where there are finely-carved canopies in memory of John Verqueray who taught at Rugby for 42 years. A sad, though fascinating story greets you at once in the west window which is inscribed: 'In memory of his father this window was erected by an Old Rugbeian in the year of 1902'. The old boy was Leonard Eaton Smith, and when he made his filial gesture he could have had no foreboding of the wording of his own ultimate memorial in the stalls below: 'Killed by enemy action while carrying out his duties as Mayor of the City of Westminster, 11 May 1941.'

Yet Rugby Chapel has a memorial to an Old Rugbeian who is the classic case of a man who seemed to know what fate had in store. In Poet's Corner in the south Transept is the eager young profile of one who was a more worthy pin-up of girls now ageing than the howling horrors favoured by their granddaughters. 'If I should die' wrote Rupert Brooke when he went to the 1914-18 War

Rugby and the Upper Avon

. . . think only this of me,
That there's some corner of a foreign field
That is forever England.

The entire sonnet is Brooke's memorial in his old school chapel—
he lies in an olive grove on the Aegean island of Scyros.

Rugby Chapel has no dim religious light. Slim cream-coloured
pillars with bands of purple rise towards a ceiling patterned in
black and white where the roof trusses spring from blue, red, and
gold corbels. Patterned red brick relieved by white bands with
black shapes, a chequered border above the transept panelling, the
blue and gold wrought ironwork hiding the organ pipes—nothing
can be disregarded. The seats face inward to the centre aisle and
there is room for the school's approximate 750 pupils. The chancel
is small compared to the nave, and again colour runs riot from the
multi-hued reredos, past the Adoration of the Magi in the sixteenth-
century glass of the east window, to the symbols of the Evangelists
in mosaic high above.

One of the striking things about Rugby memorials is the family
continuity at the school; for instance, the bronze to William
Vaughan, a boy in School House from 1879 to 1884 and 'a beloved
headmaster' from 1921 to 1931, proclaims him 'grandson, son, and
father of Rugbeians'. There are others to whom Rugby was their
whole life, like Henry Lee Warner, 'School House, Head of School,
Master under Frederick Temple, Housemaster 1875-83, and finally
Governor of the School'. Others knew little beyond Rugby because
war curtailed their young lives. Clerestory windows facing each
other across the nave commemorate those who fell in the Indian
Mutiny and those who died in the Crimean War when four Rugbeians rode at the Russian guns in the Charge of the Light Brigade.

But Rugbeians have lived too, and made great impact on our
national life—Archbishops of Canterbury like Edward Benson and
William Temple, and that greatest of Rugbeians, Thomas Arnold,
the headmaster who had such influence on public school life. A
simple stone above his grave beneath the chancel steps bears merely
his name and a cross, but he lies in effigy in the north transept. His
poet son, Matthew, is remembered in Poets' Corner. There, too, is
Arthur Hugh Clough, one of whose verses—'And not by eastern

windows only'—Churchill used to illustrate the growing power of America's war effort. Charles Lutwidge Dodgson, who as Lewis Carroll sent Alice on her adventures in Wonderland, has a memorial in the south transept featuring the Mad Hatter, the March Hare, and all their zany company.

Among the great headmasters recalled in Rugby Chapel are Tait, Percival who became Bishop of Hereford, and David who was Bishop of St. Edmondsbury, while around them cluster others who go to make up a thriving school community—a school physician, the chapel organist, and, of course, many masters, men whose precept and example moulded countless generations of boys. It is summed up in an inscription from a sermon by Bishop Percival: 'Remember them that had the rule over you, which spoke unto you the word of God, and considering the issue of their life, imitate their faith.'

Subsidiary buildings of Rugby School add lustre to the town, particularly New Big School across the road from the main block. The statue of Judge Thomas Hughes on the lawn of the Temple Reading Room is a reminder of *Tom Brown's Schooldays* which he wrote, and in Holy Trinity churchyard there is a gravestone of Thomas Thomson who died in 1885, and his wife Sarah, in 1889, servants of Dr. Arnold, mentioned in the book as Bogle and Sally.

The Oxford Canal borders Rugby to north and east, giving a water communication with London, Birmingham, and Leicester by way of Braunston. It was, however, the advent of the London and Birmingham Railway in 1838 which transformed Rugby from the busy market town for a rich agricultural district to the industrial centre it is today.

The Avon, meandering around the northern fringes of Rugby, where it receives the River Swift, has entered Warwickshire at Dow Bridge on the Watling Street (A5). Upstream it becomes the boundary between Leicestershire and Northamptonshire for some miles until it veers into the latter county where it rises near the battlefield of Naseby. Here, at the 'Fitzgerald Arms', the source of the river, Avon Well, can be seen in the garden, while in the cellar subterranean bubblings can sometimes be heard from the river. Rising near one battlefield, the Avon joins the Severn on another, at Tewkesbury, Gloucestershire, but 58 miles of its 96 miles course is in our county, and it is known as the Warwickshire Avon.

For 18 miles north-westward of Dow Bridge the Roman Watling Street is the boundary between Warwickshire and Leicestershire until, at Mancetter, the River Anker takes over. The boundary jumps from side to side of Watling Street, always a 'boothing depth' from the highway—sufficient space to build a house, but each county has nine miles of the road to maintain. Near Caves Inn Farm, a mile north of Dow Bridge, where the old London and North Eastern line crosses Watling Street, the Romans spanned three streams and called their camp Tripontium. Cave's Inn, formerly Cave's Hole, is associated with Edward Cave, born at Churchover nearby, who, in 1731, founded the *Gentlemen's Magazine*, but there has been no inn there for 70 years at least. Another mile, and Gibbet Hill was an airy place to hang a malefactor in view of a spacious landscape embracing three counties. Six more dead straight miles, and Watling Street, striking from London to Chester, crosses the Fosse Way from Bath to Lincoln at Venonae, the navel of Roman England.

Known today as High Cross, the junction is marked by the battered remains of a memorial erected by the Earl of Denbigh to celebrate the end of the War of the Spanish Succession against the French in 1712. Originally the memorial consisted of four Doric columns supporting a globe, but this was destroyed by lightning in 1791. The inscription reads: 'If, traveller, you search for the footsteps of the ancient Romans, here you may behold them; for here their most celebrated ways, crossing each other, extend to the utmost boundaries of Britain. Here the Venones had their quarters and at the distance of one mile hence Claudius, a certain Commander of a Cohort, seems to have had a camp towards the Street, and towards the Fosse a tomb '

This is the area of the 'big and little' villages which take the suffix Magna or Parva. Warwickshire has a Harborough Magna and Parva, and a Copston Magna, while Leicestershire boasts its Claybrooke Magna and Parva, Ashby Magna and Parva, Peatling Magna and Parva, Wigston Magna and Parva, and Glen Parva. Place-names also suggest a Danish influence with Wibtoft in Warwickshire and Yelvertoft in Northamptonshire.

It is open country north of Rugby and west of the Watling Street, much given to sheep rearing. Villages and great estates are few, which gives particular prominence to Monks Kirby, with Newnham

Paddox alongside the village, seat of the Earls of Denbigh until recently, but demolished in 1952. St. Edith's magnificent tower at Monks Kirby, with its powerful buttresses and four crocketed pinnacles crowned by flag vanes, dominates a wide countryside. It is an astonishing church for so insignificant a village, and until 1701 it was even more imposing, its tower being surmounted by an octagonal spire which was blown down in a great gale, an inscription in the priest's room above the porch reading: 'This roofe was beate down and the midle roof and the two side iles the 25th of December 1701. Thomas Crook, James Buswell, churchwardens; Thomas Bewley, plumber, 1702.'

A plan of the seating allotted by the commissioners in 1702 shows the private pews of the great families, the Earls of Denbigh and Sir Francis Skipwith, around the pulpit, with their servants alongside. In the nave are the pews of the farmers and others, while an area at the west end looks like 'standing room only' for 'labourers and servants'.

Monks Kirby Church is dedicated to St. Edith, the Saxon Abbess of Polesworth, daughter of King Egbert. She appears with Canute, Ethelred, and Harold in stained glass above the font. Another Saxon monarch, Edward the Confessor, is the subject of the story told in eight scenes in this window—a memorial to Edward Wood, who died in 1882 at Newbold Revel, a mansion nearby, now used as St. Paul's Roman Catholic Training College. Edward the Confessor was canonized, and is identified by the ring he holds in this window, a ring he once gave to an elderly palmer who turned out to be St. John the Divine—apparently resurrected.

Its spaciousness makes Monks Kirby Church remarkable among village churches. Free from constricting rood screen, the nave and chancel merge. In contrast to the huge tower pillars, the arcade pillars of pinkish brown rise with a slim grace and without capitals to their lofty arches.

There is a chapel at each side of the chancel. The Skipwith Chapel to the south has a tablet to Sir Gray Skipwith, Bart., one of the last of his family to live at Newbold Revel, which they sold in 1862. A hatchment hangs above with the Skipwith arms and their unusual crest, a turnstile. The north chapel may embody remains of the Benedictine monastery founded by Geoffrey de Wirce in 1077.

There, and along the north wall of the nave, are memorials of the Feilding family, the Earls of Denbigh, to whom one of the village public houses is dedicated. They, too, have an interesting crest, a nuthatch with a hazel twig in her beak. They lived at Newnham Paddox from the fifteenth century until 1952, but the seat of the 10th Earl is now Pailton House, near Rugby.

In the reign of James I a William Feilding was ennobled as the 1st Earl of Denbigh on the band-wagon of his brother-in-law, George Villiers, Duke of Buckingham, the king's favourite. The earl and the duke accompanied Charles, Prince of Wales, later Charles I, to Spain, all of them disguised, for Charles to woo the Infanta. He failed, but Basil Feilding, the earl's heir, was a more successful marriage broker, being in the mission to Paris which arranged Charles's alliance with Henrietta Maria. Earl William fought for the king in the Civil War but Basil joined the Roundheads, and father and son commanded sections on opposite sides at Edgehill. The following year the Earl died of wounds received in the Battle of Birmingham, and Roundhead son succeeded Royalist father, but though Basil married four times he had no children and the title passed to his nephew.

The 4th Earl of Denbigh was the uncle of Henry Fielding, the novelist, who must have known the spelling rule I learned in my infant school—'i before e except after c'—for he altered the spelling of his surname.

Among the Monks Kirby memorials is a touching little tablet to Mary, Countess of Denbigh, who died in 1842, from 'the peasant boys of Monks Kirby and Pailton'. Her son, Rudolph, the 8th Earl, was a convert to Roman Catholicism, and his christian name is a pointer to the descent once claimed by the Feildings from the Imperial Austrian Hapsburgs. The name Rudolph was supposed to derive from a nephew of the great Rudolph of Hapsburg—Geoffrey, Count of Rheinfelden (cf. Feilding) who came to England in the fourteenth century, married and left a son who married the heiress of Robert de Newnham of Newnham Paddox. Consequently the double-headed Hapsburg eagle appears on several Feilding monuments. When a well-known genealogist virtually disproved the claim the Feildings took it philosophically and have since called themselves the 'Perhapsburgs'.

Despite the Austrian eagle the Feildings have fought and died for Britain. Two sons of the 7th Earl became generals, the younger, William, dying of cholera in Siam in 1895, while the elder, Sir Percy, served 32 years in the Coldstream Guards and fought throughout the Crimean War, being present at Alma, Balaclava, and Inkerman, where he was severely wounded. Two more Feildings died on active service in the First World War.

Among the humbler people of Monks Kirby there died in 1720 one Elizabeth Mott, mother of 42 children. I could not find her grave, but my search was rewarded with a gem of an epitaph to Thomas Lewis, sexton for 44 years, who died in 1849:

> *The graves around for many a year*
> *Were dug by him who slumbers here;*
> *Till worn with age, he dropped his spade,*
> *And in this dust his bones are laid.*

A mile east of Monks Kirby Church, is the Newnham Paddox estate. Though the house is gone the great wrought-iron gates still stand, deserted, closed, and leading to an overgrown drive fringed with Lombardy poplars. Described as 'perhaps the largest and most beautiful in the kingdom', the gates were made by Welsh craftsmen around 1720, set up at a monastery in Spain, brought back to Berwick House, near Shrewsbury, and moved in 1873 to their present site.

Five miles northward of Monks Kirby, on Wolvey Heath, the Earl of Warwick, the 'Kingmaker', once arrested the King of England. Raising an army against the Lancastrians in 1469, Edward IV had marched from Buckinghamshire to Wolvey, where his brother-in-law, Sir Anthony Woodville, Earl Rivers, was assembling a force. There was little love in England for the family of Elizabeth Woodville, Edward's queen, and Warwick had promised the Commons that the Woodvilles would be banished.

Learning of Edward's rendezvous, Warwick led his force by night to the camp on Wolvey Heath, and there, striding from his tent in the moonlight, the king was confronted by an intimidating sight, described by Lytton in *The Last of the Barons*:

'Around the tent stood a troop of torch-bearers, and the red glare

182

29 *Buildings at Stoneleigh Abbey, home of Lord Leigh*

30 *Rugby School Chapel with the war memorial extension to the left*

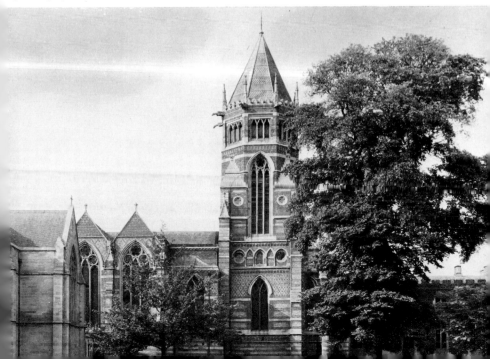

shone luridly upon the steel of the serried horsemen and the banners of the Earl, in which the grim White Bear was wrought upon an ebon ground quartered with the Dun Bull.'

Warwick had brought off a bloodless coup; Woodville's troops were unprepared. Lytton makes Warwick stern but respectful, and as he marches Edward off to Warwick Castle he still addresses him as 'King'. Shakespeare depicts a chillier relationship in *Henry VI, Part III*, Warwick referring to his captive as 'Duke'.

King Edward: 'The duke! Why, Warwick, when we parted thou call'dst me King'.

Warwick: 'Ay, but the case is altered: when you disgraced me in my embassade then I degraded you from being King, and come now to create you Duke of York.'

Warwick sent Edward into captivity at Middleham Castle, Yorkshire, but the King escaped and on 14 April 1471, Warwick was killed at Barnet fighting for the Lancastrians, and Edward came more firmly to the throne. There is no reminder in Wolvey today of this episode, but the village has a link with the Wars of the Roses in the 'Blue Pig', a version of the Blue Boar badge of the Lancastrian Earl of Oxford.

Eighty-six years after Edward's capture Wolvey Heath again glowed with flames on another exciting occasion in the history of this village on the Coventry-Leicester road. In 1555, when Bloody Mary was burning Protestants, a fire was lit on Wolvey Heath to consume the young and lovely Lady Dorothy Smyth of Shelford Manor. She had not incurred the Catholic wrath of Mary; she had merely murdered her husband, Sir Walter Smyth.

An ageing widower, Sir Walter wished to see his heir, Richard, settled now that he had come of age. So he approached Mr. Thomas Chetwynd of Ingestre, Staffordshire—'a gentleman of ancient family and fair estate' according to Dugdale—who agreed to provide a dowry of £500 along with his daughter, Dorothy. When the elderly knight saw the girl 'he became a suitor for her himself, being so captivated with her beauty', and offered not only to forego the dowry, but to pay a like sum to Chetwynd for his daughter's hand.

31 *Bow window in the saloon at Arbury Hall, near Nuneaton, home of Mr. Humphrey Fitzroy Newdegate*

Her father persuaded Dorothy to the match, but soon she was seeking solace from younger men, particularly a William Robinson of Drayton Bassett, the 22-year-old son of a wealthy London mercer. With him, her maid, and a groom, Dorothy conspired to murder her husband, but on the night William failed to appear.

The determined Dorothy pressed on without him. When Sir Walter was asleep she put a towel round his neck and made the groom lie on him to stop his struggles while she and the maid tightened the towel and 'stopt her husband's breath'. With touching faith the old knight, waking momentarily, called on his young wife, 'Help, Doll, help'. Sure that he was dead Dorothy arranged his body to feign suicide. Then, pretending to have missed her husband from his bed and gone in search, she raised the alarm with every show of grief. The funeral over, Dorothy went to London where she enjoyed herself with many young men, but neglected Robinson. The groom, her accomplice, had remained in the service of Richard Smyth, and one day in his cups he told the story of the murder. Sober next day, he stole Smyth's horse and made for Wales to take ship abroad, but Smyth had the ports watched, and the groom was brought prisoner to Warwick, On trial, he charged Richard with trying to frame his stepmother with the death of Sir Walter so that he might get her jointure, but eventually Dorothy confessed. The groom and maid were executed at Warwick and she burned at the stake on Wolvey Heath. They say a reprieve was on its way, but the messenger got lost and it arrived too late.

For three centuries the even tenor of life moved on in Wolvey undisturbed. True, in 1620 the roof of the north aisle of the church fell in. Otherwise the Jacques Charity of loaves was doled out each Christmas and Harvest Home celebrated annually and riotously at the 'Bull's Head', demolished recently to make way for a successor of the same name. It was this Harvest Home that brought Wolvey considerable excitement on the night of 12 October 1853. Suddenly, among the laughter a scream rang out. The floor was cleared, and Joseph Rowley, a popular villager aged 27, lay bleeding to death from a stab wound. His assailant got four years for manslaughter; Rowley was buried in Wolvey churchyard. His friends clubbed together for a memorial stone and asked the vicar to write an appropriate verse. This he did readily, for he disapproved of the harvest capers at the 'Bull's Head'. His lines, engraved on Rowley's head-stone before the villagers had seen them, ran:

> When Madness fires the young and gay
> To dance Life's latest, shortest hour away;
>   Do thou consider well:
> If this next step should prove my last,
> Where shall I wake when Death my die has cast?
>   In Heaven? No! in Hell

Rowley's friends resented this, so one night they crept into the churchyard with a lantern and some pumice stone, and patiently erased the last three offending words. You can see their handiwork today. The stone lies prone on the grass off the north-east corner of the church, and Joe Rowley is, happily, 'in Heaven'.

West of Wolvey, around Bedworth, the North Warwickshire coalfield reaches its easternmost point. Mining was first recorded in the county in the thirteenth century, and today the coalfield consists of five collieries in a triangle with a line between Coventry and Nuneaton as base and Tamworth as the apex, extending 25 miles from north to south and being seven miles across near Nuneaton. The coal-bearing strata are 750 feet thick in the north, decreasing to 450 feet in the south, while towards the south several seams coalesce to form the Warwickshire Thick Coal, at one point 26 feet thick. Administratively the Warwickshire coalfield is linked with the Leicestershire and South Derbyshire Coalfields as part of the South Midlands area of the National Coal Board, and four of the five collieries extant have all undergone thorough reconstruction since nationalization in 1947. Warwickshire lacked the quality ironstone which fostered the growth of coalmining in Staffordshire, but the development of canal transport from Ashby-de-la-Zouch to Coventry and then to London enabled the county's industry to compete in the capital with seaborne coal. The regular canal sequence was for pairs of narrow boats to travel up the Grand Union from the Middlesex wharves with various cargoes for Tyseley and Sampson Road, Birmingham, and to continue through the city along the notorious 'Bottom Road' to the Fazeley Canal, turning at Fazeley on to the Coventry Canal and so to the coalfield, where they would load for the mills around Watford, rejoining the Grand Union at Braunston, Northamptonshire.

In the 1970-71 financial year the output from the five collieries, employing a total of 4,965 men, was 3,207,000 tons, made up as follows: Baddesley, 1,000 employed, 638,000 tons; Birch Coppice, near Tamworth, 975 and 550,000; Coventry Colliery, Keresley, 1,250 and 799,000; Newdigate, Bedworth, 740 and 502,000; and Daw Mill, near Arley, 1,000 and 733,000. Daw Mill is the only new mine in Warwickshire, its 610 yards deep shaft being sunk in 1958-1959. Production began in 1965, and it aims to produce one million tons annually.

The River Sowe flows across Bedworth Heath to Exhall, fills the delightful moat around eighteenth-century Exhall Hall, and pursues a course round the eastern outskirts of Coventry, where industry has engulfed Foleshill Church with its memorial to Richard Parrott, who died in 1774, and who installed one of the first steam engines for pumping water out of his mine. At Wyken, where new factories have been built on the site of Craven Colliery, a great treasure was found in the church in 1956, a huge fifteenth-century painting of St. Christopher, uncovered on the north wall after being hidden behind plaster since 1547. The north wall was a traditional place for Christopher, patron saint of travellers, for he could then be seen by any passer-by glancing in at the usual south door. A medieval couplet ran:

If thou the face of Christopher on any morn shalt see,
Throughout the day from sudden death thou shalt preserved be.

Wyken's Christopher has the Christ Child on his shoulder as he fords a river. Their cloaks are billowing behind them in the breeze, and on the bank in perfect preservation is painted a post windmill, while a red-eyed fish worries the saint's leg and an octopus looks on.

Near Wyken Church was Caludon Castle, home of the Mowbrays, from where Thomas Mowbray, Duke of Norfolk, started in September 1398 for Gosford Green to his 'wager of battle' with Henry Bolinbroke, featured in Shakespeare's *Richard II*. Bolinbroke, later Henry IV, set out from Baginton Castle some five miles down the Sowe. The contestants had accused each other of treason, and Richard called them to combat only as an excuse to banish them without a blow struck, Bolinbroke for six years, Mowbray for life.

Continuing downstream with the Sowe towards Coombe Abbey we reach Binley Church, a neat little eighteenth-century essay in the Adam style, which has been described as 'in ballroom taste'. The east window is a monstrosity, but several Craven tombs are interesting. The river's showpiece is the Old Mill Inn at Baginton, where the 18-foot wheel can be seen through a glass screen in the grill room.

In its last mile the Sowe achieves the grace denied it earlier. Stoneleigh, alongside a stretch of Warwickshire's loveliest parkland, is a charming village with some striking black and white, but even better, warmer red brick and timber. It also boasts a row of tall-chimneyed almshouses, built by Alice Leigh, the only woman to be created a duchess in her own right—as Duchess Dudley by Charles I. An exquisite Norman chancel arch of pink-hued sandstone is the gem of many attractive features in Stoneleigh Church, where the Leighs of Stoneleigh Abbey are commemorated in memorials and hatchments. There is a memorial to George Jones, civil engineer, who in 1809 built the Royal Military Canal along the south-east coast against Napoleonic invasion, and the gleaming gold letters of the charity boards record the gift by Thomas Southerne, a yeoman, of £4 10s. per annum for ever towards the repair of the bridges between Stoneleigh and Stareton.

From the first of these, a sturdy concrete structure nowadays, with a wooden causeway leading above flood level to the village, is soon a lovely cottage group, where tidy lawns with fruit trees slope down to the water's edge, a scene that is for ever England. As the headquarters since 1963 of the Royal Show, Britain's premier agricultural occasion, Stoneleigh is invaded each July by farmers from all over the world and English visitors seeking a day in a rural and farming environment.

CHAPTER TEN

Nuneaton and the Coalfields

That Meriden, equidistant between Birmingham and Coventry, is a lucky village with a considerable claim to fame is borne out by the inscription on a stone on a road island beside the village green: 'This oak tree was planted at the traditional centre of England by Bernard Hornby Hunt, Chairman of Warwickshire County Council, on 24 March 1962 to mark the completion of the by-pass in 1958 whereby Meriden became a village once again.'

On this green, in the peace and quiet where lorries once roared through the village, the visitor can take his ease on the stone seat inscribed 'To the memory of Wayfarer (W. M. Robinson) 17 September 1956. His devotion to the pastime of cycling inspired many to enjoy the countryside and the open road. Erected on behalf of all cyclists by the Cyclists Touring Club.'

Within a couple of turns of the pedals stands the squat obelisk to cyclists who fell in the two World Wars, and there, on a Sunday in May each year, cyclists, though in dwindling numbers, come for a memorial service.

A wayside cross is the oldest mark of Meriden's central position, having stood in the village for 500 years. Meriden Church, up on its hill, includes among its several interesting items a set of 18 blue staves some six feet long and metal-topped, arranged fanwise in the ringing chamber. They were formerly used by members of Meriden Friendly Society at their annual service on St. John the Baptist's Day. An elaborate effigy of an unknown knight is given added interest rather than defaced by a piece of seventeenth-century vandalism, the initials M.H. and the date 1678 scratched on a leg.

The road to Fillongley and Nuneaton soon crosses the by-pass which has restored tranquillity to Meriden as it diverts the wheeled juggernaut of modern industry thundering between its various centres.

Driving on towards Fillongley one summer morning in 1970 I had the shock that comes so frequently to travellers in Warwickshire these days. It was some months since I had been that way. Suddenly the pleasant country road became unrecognizable, and, rounding a bend, I was confronted with a centipedal concrete structure carrying yet another unsuspected motorway over my head. Presumably this gives Fillongley some of the peace its by-pass bestows on Meriden, and this today is the thoughtful man's dilemma in Warwickshire more than elsewhere. Do we restore a measure of sanity and security to our villages at the expense of our agricultural acres?

Fillongley once had a Plague Stone in the churchyard. It was inscribed: 'In tempore Plage. To William Smith of Birchley Hall, buried 6 April 1623. Also 26 persons of this parish who died in the Year of Our Lord 1666. This stone is fixed here by several persons of the parish 1667.' No one seems to know why Smith was mentioned on the stone. He left orders that no one should touch his body after death, so when he fell dead out of doors he was rolled with crowbars on to a hurdle and buried in a field at Birchley Hall, a memorial stone marking the spot until it was ploughed in during the First World War. The Plague Stone has been mysteriously missing since 1940.

Fillongley is on the threshold of the George Eliot country. Born four miles away on 22 November 1819, at South Farm, Arbury, where her father Robert Evans was agent to the Newdigate estate, Mary Ann Evans wrote *Adam Bede, Romola, Silas Marner, The Mill on the Floss* and her other novels under the masculine nom-de-plume because she felt a man's writing would attract more attention. Beneath a yew south of Fillongley Church is the bulky tomb of Isaac Pearson, her uncle, a prosperous farmer.

Passing the Weavers Arms, a winding minor road climbs to wide views northward as it crosses Fillongley ridge, soon to come to Astley, where one of Warwickshire's most stirring historical occasions is scarcely remembered with a little-known monument in a potato field on Duke's Farm. No soldier on jankers ever cursed spuds more heartily than I did after hopping the rows one muddy day to the clearing surrounding the beehive-shaped mass of brown stone, where I read this legend: 'On this spot formerly stood a huge hollow oak tree in which Henry Grey, Duke of Suffolk, Lord of the Manor of Astley, the father of Lady Jane Grey, took refuge from his pursuers. He was betrayed here by his keeper, Underwood, and executed on Tower Hill, London, 12 February 1554. The tree was blown down in 1891.'

How could anyone historically-minded enough to erect this monument make a mistake in the date? 12 February was the date on which Suffolk's daughter, Lady Jane Grey, the unhappy nine-days' queen was executed with her young husband, Guildford Dudley. Suffolk was beheaded on 23 February. The erroneous date seems to be accepted with the monument, for no book nor newspaper cutting to which I have had access points out the mistake.

They are more correct at Arbury Hall nearby, where, among the historical items on show in this most charming of stately homes is the chair and table used by the duke while hiding in that oak. Here they give the proper date of his execution.

Astley Castle—scarcely of castle proportions, and now a pleasant hotel—stands across a moat from the bulky church. The moat is older than either, predating the first of three castles on the site by a century, while the present church is a seventeenth-century rebuilding of a ruin. The Greys came to the second castle when Joanne Astley, widowed in 1450, married Lord Reginald Grey of Ruthin. By his marriage a grandson of this couple, Sir John Grey, brought to Astley Castle one who was to become Queen of England even earlier than the ill-fated Jane Grey.

She was Elizabeth Woodville who, widowed when Sir John was killed fighting for the Lancastrians at St. Albans in 1461, found favour with Edward IV. It is said that she confronted the king while he was hunting in Whittlebury Forest, Northamptonshire. The Astley Estates had been forfeit to the Crown when Edward came to the throne after his victory at Towton, and Elizabeth waylaid the king to plead for their return to her two sons. Not only did Edward accede to the request; he also married Elizabeth secretly, and a year later she was crowned Queen at Westminster.

Among her many relatives given titles was her son, Sir Thomas Grey, who became Earl of Huntingdon and later the 1st Marquis of Dorset. With his wife Lady Ciceley Bonneville he lived at Astley

Castle, but built also a splendid house in Bradgate Park, near Leicester, where his unfortunate great-granddaughter, Lady Jane Grey, was to spend her childhood. With their new grandeur Queen Elizabeth and her family suffered much jealousy from the longer-established nobility, but Elizabeth's own personal tragedy was the murder by Richard III's party of her two young sons by Edward IV —Edward V and Richard of York—the 'Princes in the Tower'.

With the accession of Richard III several Greys and Woodvilles went to the block, while the Marquis of Dorset fled into exile. His wife, Ciceley, is buried at Astley, where her effigy was among many in the chancel and transept of the old church. Three only survive in the present edifice, one being Ciceley, whose reclining alabaster figure lies just inside the west door with those of Sir Edward Grey, Lord Ferrers, and his daughter-in-law Elizabeth Talbot, Lady Lisle.

Astley Church is a place of great attraction, not the least interest coming from 21 shields on the ceiling, each of a great Midlands family. Here are the two blue chevrons and ermine of the Duke of Suffolk, the manches of the Hastings, and the lions gambes of the Newdegates. Two memorials recall the struggle in the Crimea, that of Sir Henry Richard Legge Newdigate who served there with the Rifle Brigade, and one to the Rev. Robert Freeman, officiating chaplain to Her Majesty's Forces before Sebastopol, and specially attached to the immortal Light Cavalry Brigade. He survived the campaign but died on the passage home.

Among all this 'quality' is a more humble memorial: 'Here is lamented Mrs. Lettice Bolton who lived very hansomely (*sic*) upon a narrow fortune. Her life was without trouble and her death without pain. She explred suddenly the 17 February 1693/4, aged 65'— in those distant days when the calendar and legal years differed up to Lady Day, March 25.

Misericords and paintings of prophets and apostles decorate the choir stalls at Astley, and wall paintings add to the interest. Astley was the 'Knebley' of George Eliot, and there is a memorial in the church to her father's first wife, Harriet Poynton, who died in 1809. Mrs. Ann Garner, one of the novelist's three aunts who appear in *The Mill on the Floss* as the Dodson sisters, lived at Sole End Farm, Astley, and Garners cluster thick in the north of the churchyard.

After the execution of the Duke of Suffolk, Queen Mary Tudor had Astley Castle demolished, but the widowed Duchess rebuilt the present more domestic castle. She married Adrian Stokes, one of her estate workers, and he stole lead from the roof and steeple of the church, thus causing the eventual collapse of the steeple, which destroyed the entire church. It was Sir Richard Chamberlayne, on whom Queen Mary bestowed the Astley Estate when the Duchess died in 1558, who erected the present church, one fifth the size of the original, from the stones of an erstwhile side chapel. With Sir Richard's death in 1654 Astley Castle was purchased by Sir Richard Newdigate, from Arbury Hall just across the Nuneaton road.

Arbury is open to the public, and my favourite time for a visit is when the bluebells spread their thick carpet beneath the great oaks of the extensive park. The hall is not just a museum of unrelated collections of art and crafts, but a home, an integral whole where everything contributes to the saga of the Newdegate family, owners of Arbury since John Newdigate acquired it in 1586 from Edmund Anderson, giving him in exchange Harefield Place, Middlesex (A difficulty in writing of the Newdegates is their haphazard spelling with a middle 'e' or 'i', so I take the spelling for each individual from the pedigree in the Arbury guidebook.)

On my last visit I was taken back to Arbury's origins in the gallery with a deed issued by the prior and convent of Augustinian canons founded at Arbury by Ralph de Sudeley in the reign of Henry II. Here, too, is the Newdegate pedigree, sketches of the house in Elizabethan days, and letters written by Sir Christopher Wren from his London home concerning his designs for the Arbury stable doorway, for which he received a pair of silver candlesticks in part payment. Less formal social history is revealed in the entrance hall, mainly in the period of the great Sir Roger Newdigate, fifth and last baronet, and eighth of his line to own Arbury. He it was who wrought the transformation from the original Elizabethan to the existing Gothic between 1750 and 1805. Arbury Hall is George Eliot's 'Cheveral Manor' and this rebuilding the theme of *Mr. Gilfil's Love Story*, with Sir Roger her Sir Christopher Cheveral.

Sir Roger was a meticulous annotator. His monthly notes to his gardeners include instructions to 'destroy snails and vermin which will destroy your choicest fruits', and there are comments on the growing of pineapples at Arbury. Accounts of the Nuneaton Company of Militia for 1761 in Sir Roger's hand include a guinea to the drum major for 'teaching my two drummers to fife'. Some of Sir Roger's rebuilding was financed by Griff Colliery, nearby, which he owned, and his accounts show the sale of coal in one year as 2,152 tons, with considerable expenditure from 1770 to 1775 for digging a canal to link Arbury with the Coventry Canal. Later evidence of the family interest in coal peeped pleasantly above the southern horizon from Arbury until recent years—the spoil mound of Newdigate Colliery, sunk by Sir Francis Newdigate Newdegate, grandfather of the present owner of Arbury Hall, Mr. Humphrey Fitzroy Newdegate. In common with other pit mounds in the vicinity, the Newdigate heap has been partially levelled.

The eventual failure of Griff Colliery brought hard times to Arbury. General Sir Edward Newdegate found himself with only £1,000 a year to maintain the estate, so he closed the hall and became Governor-General of Bermuda, which accounts for Bermuda village on the Arbury Estate today.

An earlier Newdegate represented in the hall is Anne Fitton, wife of Sir John, and sister of Mary Fitton, Queen Elizabeth's maid of honour and probably Shakespeare's 'Dark Lady of the Sonnets'. When Mary, who was no better than she should be, was banished from Court she came to stay at Arbury, and still looks quizzically down on the dining-room from a beautiful painting. There is a letter to Anne, impeccably written by Arabella Stewart, 'hopinge this our acquaintance newlye begonne shall continewe and growe greater.' Arabella, cousin and next in succession to James I, was imprisoned by him in the Tower for marrying against his wishes.

The pansy emblem of the Fittons appears frequently among the heraldic devices at Arbury with those of other families into which the Newdegates married, including the Warwickshire Leighs.

The rooms shown to visitors to Arbury lead mainly off the 'cloisters' on the east front. First of them, the chapel, has a ceiling of exquisite Caroline plaster-work which occupied Edward Martin for four years and earned him £39.

Sir Roger, like three Newdegates before him, married twice, and the story goes that his first wife, Sophia Conyers, was untidy, as penance for which he made her embroider the stools still seen in the schoolroom. More interesting is a screen in the gallery, embroidered at the age of 84 by Elizabeth Twisden, second wife of the third baronet, Sir Richard, and her portrait looks down on her fine handiwork. The little sitting-room continues the sequence of progressively more imposing ceilings, and a portrait of Sir Richard Newdigate is the guide's occasion to explain that this second baronet started a small-arms industry in Birmingham in the late seventeenth century. Another Newdegate venture into industry was with a weaving factory at Colleycroft, near Bedworth—the 'Weavers Arms' aforementioned suggests that this was not an isolated occurrence of the craft locally.

The saloon is breathtaking, its glorious bow window giving ample light with which to revel in the magnificent fan vaulting of the ceiling, derived from Henry VII's Chapel at Westminster Abbey. With such architectural craftsmanship around, you probably will not spare a glance for Sir Joshua Reynolds' painting of John the Baptist as a boy. Here, too, George Romney adds to the Newdegate portrait gallery full-length portraits of Sir Roger and his second wife, Hester Mundy. Chelsea ware is a feature of the gracious and restful drawing-room, and the tour of Arbury ends in the dining-room, which owes its great height to its having been the entrance hall of the Elizabethan mansion.

I spent my first fortnight in the Royal Artillery in September 1940 in camp at Arbury Park. Later, German prisoners-of-war moved in, and in 1946-7 they played a major part in helping the parishioners rebuild Chilvers Coton Church, east of Arbury, which was practically destroyed by the Luftwaffe on 17 May 1941. The font where Mary Ann Evans was baptized is replaced by one fashioned from the broken church pillars by a German, Max Hatzinger. Damaged in the air raid were the memorial tablets to the Rev. Bernard Ebdell and Signor Dominico Motta of the Kingdom of Naples who resided at Arbury Hall and taught music to Hester, Lady Newdegate, and Sally Shilton—Lady Cheveral and Caterina in *Scenes of Clerical Life*. George Eliot called Chilvers Coton 'Shepperton', a name sufficiently accepted for a churchyard seat to be inscribed 'Shepperton Co-operative Women's Guild, Festival of Britain, 1951.'

Survivors of the air raid are the benefactors' boards of which George Eliot wrote in *The Sad Fortunes of the Rev. Amos Barton* that they told of 'benefactions to the poor of Shepperton with an involuted elegance of capitals and final flourishes.' The original of Amos was the Rev. John Gwyther, whose wife, Emma, lies beneath a yew at the west end of the church 'Waiting the summons of the Archangel's trumpet'. George Eliot's parents, Robert and Christiania Evans, are also buried at Chilvers Coton, immediately south of the figure of the 'Resurrected Christ.'

Occasionally a church retains the hour-glass above the pulpit from which the preacher—and the congregation—could measure the duration of the sermon. Chilvers Coton pulpit is more subtle. Carved on it is a representation of St. Paul's marathon sermon at Troas from Acts, 20—'And there sat in a window a certain young man named Eutychus ... and as Paul was long preaching he sunk down with sleep and fell from the third loft and was taken up dead.'

Chilvers Coton is a suburb of Nuneaton, a busy market town of nearly 60,000 with textile and other industries at the centre of the North Warwickshire coalfield. Nuneaton is George Eliot's 'Milby', and the Newdegate Arms Hotel her 'Oldinport Arms'. With the opening of the George Eliot Memorial Gardens in 1952 the annual memorial service was transferred from Arbury Chapel to Nuneaton, while Arbury also shifted another George Eliot incubus to Nuneaton, the obelisk beside the Anker. This river comes down from Leicestershire by way of Burton Hastings, where a lane runs from the church across the Ashby Canal by a hump-backed bridge to end at Burton Mill, where Mr. John Morris maintains a family milling tradition stretching back to 1849.

His father was born at Walsgrave-on-Sowe Mill to southward, while one grandfather had windmills at Warton and Grendon north-west of Burton Hastings. An uncle was born at Tuttle Hill Wind-mill, near Nuneaton, moving to Bilstone Mill on the River Sence in Leicestershire, and another uncle worked Wolston Mill, near Coventry. Formidable—but this countryside was once liberally dotted with windmills, Wolvey having 27 in the Middle Ages. Standing beside the picturesque millpool above his house and orchard Mr. Morris told me that the water-wheel develops 60 h.p. driving two mills, the oat-crusher, and the lifting tackle, though he also has four electric mills. In winter sufficient head of water is kept by the dam to work the wheel for 12 hours, but in dry weather the mill works only until mid-day. Up steep stairs we came to the 'works' where the cogs are made of hard apple wood, the mill-stones being dressed every three months.

From Burton Mill the Anker meanders three meadowland miles to Nuneaton, flanking, at Attleborough, a housing estate where so much glass is used in the construction of the buildings that it is embarrassing to walk around it. Since the 1890s a firm of worsted spinners has occupied Anker Mill near Attleborough Road bridge, originally a cotton-spinning mill established around 1860 to relieve unemployment. Flotillas of ducks dabble on the Anker as it flows through Riversley Park beside Nuneaton Art Gallery, the town's war memorial, and the many-storeyed Nuneaton Flour Mill, which has followed the usual pattern of surviving water mills, eventually installing an oil engine, then electric power. Flour milling ceased in 1959, and now only animal fodder compounds are produced.

The Anker flows beneath a department store in Nuneaton town centre, to emerge where a modern sculptor has perpetrated an angular and nasty monstrosity of two boys wrestling. Queen Victoria looks unblushingly at their nakedness across Bond Gate, but is probably not amused.

St. Mary's Church in Manor Court Road embodies remains of the church of the Benedictine Nunnery, founded in the twelfth century, which gave the prefix to the town around it, originally called Eaton. At the Dissolution Henry VIII granted the nunnery to Sir Marmaduke Constable, whose effigy lies recumbent in the impressive parish church of St. Nicholas, his head resting on a helmet with a fully-rigged ship as the crest.

Towards Weddington the river gives its name to a public house, the Anker Inn, which must cause raised eyebrows among passers-by whose spelling is stronger than their knowledge of local topography. Weddington Hall is gone, but Caldecote Hall still stands two miles downstream brooding on its memories. Caldecote's great day came on 28 August 1642 when Mrs. Joane Purefoy and her domestics defended the house against Prince Rupert who had come to capture the squire, Colonel Purefoy. He was not at home, and thus lived to become one of the regicides who signed the death warrant of Charles I. A soldier and lawyer, William Purefoy travelled much in Europe, and it was in Geneva in 1611 that he gave serious thought to the overthrow of the monarchy in England. He became M.P. for

Coventry and was Sheriff of Warwickshire in 1631 when his puritan outlook made him the scourge of alehouse rowdies. In 1640 he became M.P. for Warwick in the Long Parliament, and was in arms against King Charles from the start of the Civil War. While in command of Parliamentary troops at Warwick Castle in 1642 he caused much damage to the Beauchamp Chapel in St. Mary's, and his men broke down the cross in Warwick market place while Purefoy stood by encouraging them. For this iconoclasm he was paid £1,500 by Parliament.

According to 'Hard Pressed, A Ballad of Old Caldecote' by a local versifier, A. F. Cross, it was 'a smiling Sabbath morn' when Prince Rupert with his brother Prince Maurice came looking for Colonel Purefoy. Beneath Tuttle Hill their troops conferred on how best to attack the manor house, a conference that would surely have been short had they known how few were the defenders. Joane Purefoy was lucky in having at Caldecote her son-in-law, George Abbot, who, when exhorted to surrender

> *Made answer there and then,*
> *'"Tis only cowards flee:*
> *God and the Right are on our side*
> *Who'll fight along o' me?"'*

Such brave words deserved a more formidable force than Abbot could muster—eight serving men, Mrs. Purefoy, and her maids, with 12 muskets. These the men fired as the maids loaded, with such good effect that when the Royalists broke down the main gate of the outer courtyard three of their officers and several soldiers were killed. Around 4 p.m. Rupert was repelled again, but in the evening he set fire to the outhouses and attacked under cover of darkness and smoke. The stratagem was unnecessary, the household's ammunition being entirely spent. Surprised at the meagre garrison Rupert proved gallant in victory, refusing his men any plunder, praising Mrs. Purefoy for her spirit, and offering George Abbot a high command if he would join the Royalists.

George declined. His memorial in Caldecote Church refers to his defence of the hall, but waxes equally eloquent about 'his perspicacious paraphrases on the Books of Job and the Psalms.' Colonel

Purefoy's military career continued in the defence of Coventry and in marauding operations in the Midland counties. After the execution of King Charles, Purefoy remained in politics and the army, finally commanding the forces in Warwickshire against the 'New Royalist' rising of Sir George Booth. A month later Purefoy was dead, and his estates were forfeited to the Crown at the Restoration. Still bearing the scrolled motto above the entrance—*Vince Lalum Patentia*, 'Evil is conquered by patience', Caldecote Hall is now divided into flats, but there is evidence of its defence in the door of the church nearby. Originally the door of the hall, it is pitted with Royalist bullet holes.

Two miles further down the Anker, at Mancetter Church, there is a splendid bit of mickey-taking, albeit unwitting. In the north aisle among memorials to the Bracebridge family of Atherstone Hall is one to Charles Holte Bracebridge, last of the line, who died in 1872. His inscription claims his descent 'in direct male line from Peter de Bracebridge, Lord of Kingsbury in the reign of King John, and on the female side from Egbert, first King of England, and Alfred the Great, from the Plantagenet kings and John of Gaunt, from the ancient kings of Scotland and Robert Bruce, and from the ancient earls of Mercia, Warwick, and Northumberland.'

Twenty yards distant in the churchyard, as though to rebuke such pride, is a mysterious little stone inscribed:

> *Here lieth interr'd*
> *the Bodys of*
> *I*
> *H.I.M.*
> *What Ere we was or am*
> *it matters not.*
> *To whome related*
> *or by whome begott.*
> *We was but am not,*
> *Ask no more of me;*
> *'Tis all we are*
> *And all that you must be.*

This intriguing stone is certainly older than the Bracebridge eulogy.

It stands back to back with one to Ann Beale, who died in 1765, which declares her 'a loving wife, a tender mother, a good mistress, and a quiet neighbour'.

Manor house and church are neighbours at Mancetter, the churchyard competing in season with the manor gardens in colourful beauty. Add to this the abundant interest of its headstones on the well-kept turf, and you have possibly the most attractive churchyard in Warwickshire. I could read in comfort every headstone there; in most churchyards a painfully damp occupation with rain or dew on the long grass. Leicestershire's Swithland slate, as workable as it is durable, accounts for most of these memorials, so that the inscriptions are masterpieces of the stonemason's art. Brown of Nuneaton, T. Coulson of Barwell, Kennell and Haddon of Atherstone, Fox, Spencer, and W. Tabbener; all proudly sign their craftsmanship. Who, I wonder, composed the verses on most of these slate headstones, a whole treasury of them, better in bulk than epitaphs anywhere in Britain?

Mancetter Church is as intriguing as the churchyard. Another reproof to the illustrious Charles Bracebridge might be seen in the motto of the Baxter family *Virtute non Verbia*, 'Virtue not Words'. Springing from a Richard Baxter, a seventeenth-century town clerk of Lichfield, the family numbered a Michael Posthumous Baxter among them, the Posthumous showing him to have been born after the death of his father.

The pride of Mancetter Church is its two martyrs, Robert Glover and Joyce Lewis, whose stories are told on tablets. Robert, and his brothers William and John, who owned the manor house, were staunch adherents of the reformed faith, a bold stand to take in the reign of Bloody Mary. In 1555 the Bishop of Lichfield ordered the Mayor and Sheriff of Coventry to arrest them, but the friendly mayor gave warning in time for William and John to escape, leaving Robert, bedridden with sickness, to be captured in what has come to be known as the 'Martyr's Bedroom'. Still the mayor tried to prevent the arrest, later pleading with Glover to offer bail, but this he steadfastly refused to do. Questioned by the Bishop, he was thrust into a dungeon at Lichfield and orders given for him to be burned at the stake on 20 September 1555. For some days he was deeply depressed, feeling that the Lord had forsaken him, but, says the account in

Mancetter Church, 'as he drew near to the stake he was on a sudden so mightily replenished with Holy comfort and Heavenly joy that he clapped his hands and exclaimed "He is come, He is come" '.

Joyce Lewis was the wife of Thomas Lewis who lived at Manor Farm beside the manor house. A strict Catholic, she was 'led by the cruel persecutions of the Church of Rome to doubt whether it could be the Church of Christ', and, as a friend of John Glover, she was further revolted by Robert's martyrdom. Behaving 'irreverently' in church, she was served with a citation by the Bishop of Lichfield, which her husband forced the messenger to eat. Failing thereafter in his resolution, Thomas Lewis brought Joyce to trial when threatened with £100 fine. She was imprisoned for 12 months, and on 18 December 1557 burned at Lichfield. Her memorial at Mancetter declares: 'When chained to the stake she manifested a cheerful serenity and a countenance so unchanged as to astound all who beheld her, and when the flames burned around her, standing unmoved. She only lifted up her hands to Heaven, whither her triumphant spirit speedily ascended.'

Atherstone, in common with Meriden and Fillongley, has been saved from ordeal by traffic with the coming of its by-pass, and its pub signs overhanging the narrow Watling Street barely a mile north-westward of Mancetter are now less likely to be borne away on tall passing pantechnicons. This was once the fate of the 'Hat and Beaver' sign, a reminder that the beaver was once prevalent in Britain and its fur much in demand for Atherstone's principal industry—hatting.

Drop down into Atherstone by the B4116 from Coleshill and the boundary wall of Merevale Hall accompanies you on your left. In the bad old days slave traders were obliged to provide hats for the slaves, and the Atherstone hatters made them. With slave emancipation in 1843 this lucrative order ceased, and from prosperity Atherstone fell into distress and unemployment, the Merevale wall being a relief measure to provide work for the unemployed hatters.

Hats have been made in Atherstone from medieval times, three factors contributing to the growth of the industry. It was handy for the wool from Leicestershire's abundant sheep; it was fairly close to Coventry which made ribbons to embellish the hats; and it was on Watling Street, a main trade highway. Hat-making is too intricate ever to have been a purely cottage industry, but from 1700 there grew up a number of small hat factories, of which about 30 remained when amalgamation began in 1890, resulting today in less than half a dozen, employing 1,000 of the town's 6,000 population. Fur hats are made mainly in Stockport, Atherstone specializing in felt hats.

Situated on the Watling Street, several Atherstone hostelries were coaching inns, and a milestone outside the 'Red Lion' gives the distance to London as exactly 100 miles. The 'Three Tuns' has on its sign reference to the Battle of Bosworth, six miles across the Leicestershire border in a countryside of large fields, the territory of the Atherstone Hunt, which has its kennels at Witherley across the Watling Street from Mancetter, where, between the two villages, the Anker takes over as the Warwickshire-Leicestershire boundary for three miles.

Beside the Anker bridge at Grendon stands Croft House, once the home of Harry Atherton Brown, a famous amateur steeplechaser. Third in the Grand National in 1920, Brown was second in 1921. Among his friends was the Duke of Windsor who, as Prince of Wales, often stayed at Croft House while hunting, and cantered his host's horses in fields beside the river. Grendon Hall, which once graced the riverside across the Polesworth road, is demolished, but its church remains with nine finely-preserved hatchments of the Chetwynds who died between 1686 and 1869. There is, too, in Grendon Church, the largest Table of Kindred and Affinity I have ever seen, reaching the full height of the north wall.

From its park like environment at Grendon the Anker approaches Polesworth through a landscape reclaimed from open-cast mining, now giving a pleasant outlook from the obelisk across the road which marks the site of St. Leonard's Chapel at Hoo, destroyed by Henry VIII in 1538. Thatched and picturesque in black and white, 'Little Jim's Cottage' stood hereabouts at St. Helena, Polesworth's eastern suburb, until its demolition in 1971. 'Little Jim', a tear-jerking ballad in the George R. Sims style, was the best-known production of Edward Farmer, a railway detective, who died in 1876. It began :

The cottage was a thatched one, the outside old and mean,
Yet everything within that cot was wondrous neat and clean;
The night was dark and stormy, the wind was howling wild,
A patient mother sat beside the deathbed of her child;
A little worn-out creature, whose once-bright eyes were dim,
It was a collier's only child; they called him Little Jim.

It is said that Farmer was going one night from Polesworth to Dordon Hall when he sought shelter from a blizzard in the isolated miner's cottage where Little Jim was dying, and this inspired his poem.

Industrial Polesworth has an unexpectedly charming backwater where, though the abbey is gone, its gatehouse still embodying Norman fabric leads to the church which has some fine Norman arcading. It was in the ninth century that Egbert, then King of Wessex, built a convent at Polesworth in gratitude to Modwena, a saintly Irish princess who cured his son of leprosy. She became a nun, and was joined by Egbert's daughter at Polesworth—the Edith to whom Polesworth Church is dedicated, for both ladies were canonized and St. Modwena is the dedication at Burton-on-Trent. When, after the Conquest, Marmion, Lord of Tamworth, seized the nuns' estate at Polesworth, a St. Edith is said to have appeared to him in a dream and wounded him with a crozier, so that he rapidly restored the abbey which survived until its suppression under Henry VIII. This Edith was the sister of Athelstan and wife of Sitric the Dane. She too took up the religious life, and is patron of Tamworth Church.

'History and legend combine together around the name of Edith, making it difficult to disentangle the lives of three saints who bore the name in Saxon times'; thus says the Polesworth Church guide-book. The third of the trio is St. Edith of Wilton, but it is certainly Edith and her father Egbert who appear in a west window at Polesworth.

Shakespeare has boomed, but his Warwickshire contemporary, Michael Drayton, is scarcely remembered in Polesworth where he lived. Past the site of a one-time mill the Anker rates a ten-arch bridge as it flows through the town to Alvecote Pools, two miles downstream, where mining subsidence has widened the river into sheets of water so attractive as to have become preserved as a bird-watchers' paradise and a resort of anglers who have taken pike exceeding 20 lb.

North of the Anker Warwickshire thrust a salient for six miles between Staffordshire and Leicestershire to its northernmost point, only a mile south of Derbyshire. This is quiet agricultural country-side, much given to white-faced Leicester sheep and Friesian cattle, with potatoes a main crop. Farms lap up to the half dozen or so villages where healthy farmyard odours often waft out through gates and archways.

Austrey has an especially graceful broach spire. Shuttington Church, with Norman work, has a wide view from its hillock including Alvecote Pools. A prominent spire at Seckington attracts the visitor to the spot where Ethelbald, King of Mercia, set in heroic but tyrannic mould, was murdered by his thanes in 757. Almost hidden by trees, but identifiable to the practised eye, alongside the Tamworth road is an earthwork where once a Norman castle stood. Above the main lights of the east window at Seckington a St. Edith is joined by another royal Saxon who became an abbess and was canonized, St. Werburgha. A fourteenth-century chapel has a fine monument to one of Queen Elizabeth's counsellors, Robert Burdett, with kneeling figures at either side of a prie-dieu.

The king commemorated in the name of Newton Regis, Warwick-shire's most northerly parish, is Henry II, that wise Plantagenet who brought England out of the worst anarchy of the feudal system. The church tower was begun in his time, and its north-east buttress has a squint through which one may peep from the exterior. A mile north of the village, on the Tamworth-Ashby road, stands the Four Counties Inn, its sign showing the badges and outlines of Derbyshire, Leicestershire, Staffordshire, and Warwickshire, which once met at a stone in a fireplace there. Derbyshire has since receded a mile northward to the River Mease. The inn itself is in Warwick-shire, the road outside in Leicestershire, the general rate and excise are paid to Warwickshire, the water rate to Staffordshire, the phone bill to Leicestershire, and, just to keep up the four counties illusion, the inn sometimes comes under the brewery's Derby office.

The hamlet where the 'Four Counties' is located is No Man's Heath, one of those occasional areas of no man's land at a junction of counties, the resort of malefactors, prize fighters, and cock fight promoters in days when they found instant refuge from the law by dodging into a neighbouring county.

And, in this judicial limbo—with thanks for your company around my native county—I leave you.

Index

Numerals in *italic* refer to illustration numbers

Index

Index

Index

Index

Index

Index